Maximum Cool: 250 Anecdotes

David Bruce

Published by David Bruce, 2023.

While every precaution has been taken in the preparation of this book, the publisher assumes no responsibility for errors or omissions, or for damages resulting from the use of the information contained herein.

MAXIMUM COOL: 250 ANECDOTES

First edition. March 18, 2023.

Copyright © 2023 David Bruce.

ISBN: 979-8215871140

Written by David Bruce.

Table of Contents

Dedication

Dedicated to My Brother Frank

Frank was reluctant to write the words below, but he did at my request because it's an opportunity to show that people still do good deeds. This can help restore people's faith in humanity.

"I've put some thought into this, and here a few Good Deeds I've done.

"I've bought breakfast more than once for complete strangers at my favorite local diner (Tommy's Diner) just because they looked like they could use a free meal.

"A woman came into Tommy's Diner, looking like she could use a decent meal and would appreciate it being free. I watched as she walked through the restaurant and sat down. I thought to myself, 'Buy her lunch.' I fought the urge and told myself no. I looked at her after she ordered and received her meal and thought to myself, 'Buy her lunch.' Again, I told myself no. She is a complete stranger, and money is hard to come by for me as well as everyone else. I was in line at the check-out waiting to pay my bill. She came up and got into line behind me and I thought to myself, 'Buy her lunch!' I looked at her, she looked at me, I reached out and grabbed her ticket, but she didn't want to let go. I told her sort of sternly, 'I don't know why, but I really, really want to pay for your lunch. I know we are complete strangers, but I feel like I am supposed to pay for your lunch. Will you please give me the pleasure of paying for this?' She almost cried, but she did allow me the pleasure.

"In Columbus, Ohio, almost always someone is at the gas station wanting money. One day this guy asked for money. I asked him, 'Why do you want money?' He said he's hungry. (If you don't know, Speedway has hotdogs and other food and drink items.) I said, 'Come inside, I'll buy you something to eat.' He was a really nice guy. His name was Dave, and he was an Army veteran; he may have been a little mentally ill after serving in the military. He talked to me about the war (don't know what war) and how he was over there fighting bulldozers. I think a couple of hotdogs and a hot coffee made his day. It really put a smile on his face. I ended up liking this guy and I'd look for him when I was getting gas so I could help him out.

"One time a guy came in the restaurant selling an old leather jacket for $10.00 so he could get some gas. It didn't fit me, and I didn't want it anyway, but I bought it and then donated the jacket.

"A woman was driving her car with the alarm going off, so I helped her figure out how to turn it off. She had the key fob, so I'm sure she didn't steal the car.

"These are a few of the good deeds I've had the pleasure of doing."

***

The doing of good deeds is important. As a free person, you can choose to live your life as a good person or as a bad person. To be a good person, do good deeds. To be a bad person, do bad deeds. If you do good deeds, you will become good. If you do bad deeds, you will become bad. To become the person you want to be, act as if you already are that kind of person. Each of us chooses what kind of person we will become. To become a good person, do the things a good person does. To become a bad person, do the things a bad person does. The opportunity to take action to become the kind of person you want to be is yours.

Human beings have free will. According to the Babylonian Niddah 16b, whenever a baby is to be conceived, the Lailah (angel in charge of contraception) takes the drop of semen that will result in the conception and asks God, "Sovereign of the Universe, what is going to be the fate of this drop? Will it develop into a robust or into a weak person? An intelligent or a stupid person? A wealthy or a poor person?" The Lailah asks all these questions, but it does not ask, "Will it develop into a righteous or a wicked person?" The answer to that question lies in the decisions to be freely made by the human being that is the result of the conception.

A Buddhist monk visiting a class wrote this on the chalkboard: "EVERYONE WANTS TO SAVE THE WORLD, BUT NO ONE WANTS TO HELP MOM DO THE DISHES." The students laughed, but the monk then said, "Statistically, it's highly unlikely that any of you will ever have the opportunity to run into a burning orphanage and rescue an infant. But, in the smallest gesture of kindness — a warm smile, holding the door for the person behind you, shoveling the driveway of the elderly person next door — you have committed an act of immeasurable profundity, because to each of us, our life is our universe."

In her book titled I HAVE CHOSEN TO STAY AND FIGHT, comedian Margaret Cho writes, "I believe that we get complimentary snack-size portions of the afterlife, and we all receive them in a different way." For Ms. Cho, many of her snack-size portions of the afterlife come in hip hop music. Other people get different snack-size portions of the afterlife, and we all must be on the lookout for them when they come our way. And perhaps doing good deeds and experiencing good deeds are snack-size portions of the afterlife.

Front Cover Photograph for *Maximum Cool*:

Copyright: https://pixabay.com/photos/portrait-girl-graffiti-model-4599553/

Good advice for all of us: Maintain Maximum Cool.

***

This is a short, quick, and easy read.

Anecdotes are usually short humorous stories. Sometimes they are thought-provoking or informative, not amusing.

***

Educate Yourself

Read Like A Wolf Eats

Be Excellent to Each Other

Books Then, Books Now, Books Forever

***

Do you know a language other than English? If you do, I give you permission to translate this book, copyright your translation, publish or self-publish it, and keep all the royalties for yourself. (Do give me credit, of course, for the original book.)

Chapter 1: From Activism to Comedians

Activism

• On March 26, 1904, during a strike by miners in Colorado, union organizer Mother Jones was arrested on the orders of governor James P. Peabody, put on a train, taken to the border of Colorado, dropped off, and told never to return again. She took the first train possible back to Denver, then wrote Governor Peabody, "Mr. Governor, You notified your dogs of war to put me out of the state. ... I wish to notify you, governor, that you don't own the state. ... I am right here in the capital ... four or five blocks from your office. I want to ask you, governor, what in Hell are you going to do about it?"[1]

• Maury Maverick, Jr., a lawyer and columnist, was a politician for a while and served in the Texas House of Representatives in the 1950s — the time of Joseph McCarthy, who used fear of Communism to censor people and keep them quiet. When a bill was introduced to invite Senator McCarthy to speak to the Texas legislature, Mr. Maverick introduced another bill that invited Mickey Mouse to speak — on the grounds that "if we are going to invite a rat, why not a good rat?"[2]

Actors

• Some actors are modest about their success. When he was asked about the secret of his success, Alfred Lunt once replied, "I speak in a clear voice and try not to bump into the furniture." Claude Rains, one of the wonderful supporting actors in *Casablanca*, once said, "I learn the lines and pray to God." According to Boris Karloff, whose most famous role was Frankenstein's monster, "You could heave a brick out of a window and hit ten actors who could play my parts. I just happened to be on the corner at the right time."[3]

• When Marilyn Monroe and Jane Russell were invited to put their footprints in concrete outside Grauman's Chinese Theater, Ms. Monroe noticed that Jimmy Durante had left an imprint of his famous nose and Betty Grable had left an imprint of one of her famous legs.

Thinking of what she and Ms. Russell were famous for, she suggested that she sit on the wet concrete and that Ms. Russell lean forward and allow the front of her sweater to make an imprint. Unfortunately, Ms. Monroe's suggestion was vetoed.[4]

• Occasionally, actors do miss cues. Hugh Manning once found himself alone on stage after an actor missed his cue. The only available props were a piano, which he didn't know how to play, and a vase of daffodils. He sat at the piano, ran his fingers along the keys, then smelled the daffodils. Not knowing what else to do to entertain the audience until his fellow actor appeared, he ate a daffodil. The audience laughed, and for the rest of the run of the play, Mr. Manning ate a daffodil on stage each night.[5]

• When Honor Blackman, who played Mrs. Cathy Gale, left the TV series *The Avengers*, Peter Graham Scott directed the auditions for her replacement. He had met Diana Rigg, who became Mrs. Emma Peel on *The Avengers*, earlier at a New Year's Eve party. The party was crowded, someone knocked a plate of sandwiches from his hand, he bent over to retrieve them, and lying underneath the piano was Diana Rigg, who said, "Hello. How are you?"[6]

• Mrs. Patrick Campbell was very capable of being insulting when she disliked something, even while on stage. During the famous screen scene in Richard Brinsley Sheridan's *School for Scandal*, Mrs. Campbell felt that Fred Terry and William Farren were acting too slowly. Despite being on stage behind the screen in the role of Mrs. Teazle, Mrs. Campbell suddenly shouted, "Oh, do get on, you old pongers!"[7]

• In 1940 at the Old Vic, Harley Granville-Barker unofficially directed *King Lear*, meaning he did the preparatory work but would not allow his name to be announced as director. John Gielgud played King Lear, and he read through the entire play for Mr. Granville-Barker. After hearing the reading, Mr. Granville-Barker told Mr. Gielgud, "You got two lines right. Now we will begin to work."[8]

• After Jackie Chan became a big movie star in Hong Kong, he went "Hollywood." He wore a different Rolex watch for each day of the week, and to show what a big star he was and what he could get away with, he walked into an elegant Hong Kong hotel — wearing only his shorts.[9]

Ad-libs

• The late-night talk-show hosts are frequently witty. When Johnny Carson failed to properly make a pretzel out of a length of dough, the lady leading the demonstration handed him another length of pizza dough, saying, "Try this piece. I don't think yours is long enough." Johnny replied, "Yes, I think I've heard that before." Michael Jordan once appeared with David Letterman after the NBA had banned his black-and-red Air Jordan basketball shoes because they didn't have any white. David quipped, "Neither does the NBA."[10]

• Dorothy Lamour had a tough time making the Road movies with Bob Hope and Bing Crosby. Ms. Lamour memorized the script, but Mr. Hope and Mr. Crosby hired writers to come up with extra gags and ad-libs for their characters. Once, during a lengthy scene in which Mr. Hope and Mr. Crosby ignored the script, Ms. Lamour finally said, "Hey, boys — will you please let me get my line in?"[11]

Advertising

• Wendy's founder Dave Thomas once said in an interview why he had founded the fast-food chain Wendy's. He said that he was "tired of going into fast service restaurants where the pickle was bigger than the hamburger. I wanted to know where the beef was." A famous TV commercial illustrated that at Wendy's the customers can choose the toppings, while at some other fast-food restaurants, the customers cannot. In the commercial, a female Russian model keeps coming down the runway wearing the same clothing for dayvear — as the Russian-accented announcer pronounces the word — eveningvear (the model wears the same outfit, but holds a flashlight), and beachvear (the model wears the same outfit, but holds a beach ball). An interesting bit of trivia is that the female Russian model was played by a man: Howard Fishler. Another interesting bit of trivia is that the Russian lettering that can be seen on a banner displayed on the promenade said, "Keeping your teeth clean at all times is important."[12]

• Glenhall Taylor once worked with a substitute radio announcer. Very carefully, he taught the announcer how to speak the commercial for Grape Nuts cereal. However, on the air, the announcer said, "Be sure to buy grapefruit."[13]

Age

• Long after playing John Steed in *The Avengers*, actor Patrick Macnee was vacationing in California, where an elderly woman offered him a drive. Upon arrival, the elderly woman ran her fingers through his hair, pushed a button that lowered the backs of their seats, then, as Mr. Macnee writes, "She proceeded to behave with great mischief." Afterward, Mr. Macnee was relaxing when someone pointed a gun at him through the car window. His naked partner looked up and said, "Good evening, officer. How can I help you?" The police officer withdrew his gun, then told his partner, "Relax, Al. It's only a couple of oldies having a final fling."[14]

• Some women subtract a few years from their age to make themselves seem younger than they are, but Chrissie Hynde of the Pretenders adds a couple of years. Why? She is a vegetarian, and she figures that if she says that she is older than she really is, people will look at her and think about vegetarianism, "Maybe there's something in it." But if she were to subtract a couple of years from her age, people might look at her and say, "Well, it hasn't done *her* any favors."[15]

• A woman objected to buying a Renaissance painting of a young girl because it had been restored. Lord Duveen told her, "My dear Madam, if you were as old as this young girl, you would have to be restored, too."[16]

Alcohol

• When Wilson Mizner married a rich society widow, he inherited her late husband's clock collection — 2,000 clocks were kept in the Clock Room, and Mr. Mizner ordered the servants to wind the clocks and keep them in good order, despite the deafening racket they made each hour as they chimed, rang, or otherwise announced the time. Mr. Mizner enjoyed inviting hungover friends to visit the Clock Room just before the hour.[17]

• Once there was a friendly rivalry between two composers of operas: Christoph Willibald Gluck and Niccolo Piccinni. In a contest, they were each commissioned to compose an opera based on the same play by Euripides. When the two operas were performed, Gluck's was the greater success — unfortunately for Piccinni, on opening night his soprano was falling-down drunk.[18]

• During World War I, English actor Stanley Holloway served as a minor officer. During training on friendly soil, he was stationed at the rear of the men as they went on a hike. Growing thirsty a few miles into the hike, he and a friend left the men and ducked into a nearby hotel bar. When the men passed the hotel again on their way home, Mr. Holloway and his friend rejoined the hike.[19]

• We owe so much to the ancient Greeks, who invented tragedy, the theater, history, biography, philosophy, the Olympics, political theory, atomic theory, etc. A Greek poet by the name of Terpandros who lived in the middle of the 7th century B.C.E. was even credited by the poet Pindar with inventing the drinking song.[20]

• In Scotland, it is customary to offer a workman a drink when he finishes some job around your home. A woman once asked a workman if he wanted a drink after he finished a job. He was amenable, so she asked how he liked his drink. He replied, "Half whiskey and half water — and put in plenty of water."[21]

• While dining with friends, playwright Richard Brinsley Sheridan asked, "Gentlemen, are we to drink like men or beasts?" The answer was unanimous — they were to drink like men. "Right, let's get drunk," Mr. Sheridan said. "Beasts always know when they've had enough."[22]

• Lord Carson once cross-examined a witness who was known to like alcohol. He asked, "Should I be right in calling you a heavy drinker?" The witness replied, "That is my business." Lord Carson then asked, "Any other business?"[23]

Animals

• Art Linkletter is famous in part because of his interviews with children. For example, when he asked a small girl what pets she had, she replied, "I've got a dog — and I used to have chickens, ducks, and rabbits." He then asked, "Where are the chickens, ducks, and rabbits now?" She told him, "In the freezer."[24]

• Some dogs are addicted to the game of Fetch the Ball. Amber, Jane Smiley's dog, is so addicted that she plays the game by herself. Amber carries a ball to the top of the stairs, throws the ball down the stairs, and then chases and retrieves it, only to play the game again.[25]

Apologies

• When writer Ben Hecht was a young boy, his grandmother Tante Chasha took him to the Yiddish theater. All went well until a certain point in the play being performed on stage — one character was accused of stealing a diamond bracelet that had been stolen by another character. This outraged young Ben, and he began shouting for the police on stage to arrest the correct character. Ushers came running, and Ben and his grandmother were taken to the lobby, where the theater manager demanded an apology from Ben's grandmother. She replied, "Yes, I owe you an apology and here it is." Then she hit the theater manager with her umbrella. Later, she told Ben: "Remember when you grow up — that's the only way to apologize."[26]

• Peter Ustinov once laughed at one of his own jokes, then apologized, "I don't laugh at my own jokes unless they're very good. That one was particularly good."[27]

Art

• Pop artist Andy Warhol knew many wild and crazy people. A woman visitor to his factory once asked if she could shoot some of his art. Assuming that she wanted to use a camera to shoot some photographs of his art, he gave her permission. She then pulled out a small gun and shot a bullet through some of his paintings of Marilyn Monroe. Andy was surprised by the woman's action, but he repaired the paintings and sold them with the new titles *Shot Red Marilyn* and *Shot Blue Marilyn*.[28]

• During World War II, Pablo Picasso managed to continue making art, often from scrap items. A famous example is his 1943 work of art, *Bull's Head*, which is made from a bicycle seat and handlebars. In addition, friends diverted metal into Picasso's workshop, even under the eyes of Nazi guards. They hauled in the metal in crates of garbage and they hauled out the finished works of art using the same means.[29]

Baseball

• Dodger manager Charlie Dressen watched over his players carefully and enforced discipline, including a curfew. One night, he returned to the hotel late — as manager, he had no curfew — only to be told by the elevator operator, "Mr. Dressen, you have some great young men playing for you. See this baseball? I took three of your players up to the sixth floor just minutes ago. They all signed this baseball." Mr. Dressen looked at the three names on the baseball, and the next day he fined each of those three players $100.[30]

• Casey Stengel had a brother by the name of Grant who was a very good baseball player, especially when potatoes were involved. When Grant was a kid, he once put a potato in his pocket before playing a baseball game. Grant's pitcher tried to pick off a base runner but failed, so Grant threw a potato — not the baseball — back to the pitcher. When the base runner took a lead off base, Grant took the baseball out of his glove and told the base runner, "I have something to show you."[31]

Children

• First-grade students often have a very poor conception of age. One first-grader asked his teacher — she was 22 — how old she was. In turn, she asked, "How old do you think I am?" He replied, "Sixty." When she told him that he was wrong, the student asked, "More or less?" (In an Ohio classroom, a teacher told her students about General Sherman's march through the South and the devastation he wrought. One of her students asked, "Where did you hide?")[32]

• American artist Robert Motherwell was tone deaf, so he was unable to dance and sing well as a child. However, his kindergarten teacher noticed that he enjoyed painting and coloring books, so she asked him if he would like to do those things while the other children were dancing and singing. He replied, "Would I!" — then he started developing his skills as an artist.[33]

• Maria Tallchief's father owned a pool hall, and as the daughter of the owner, young Maria was entitled to free candy from the pool hall. However, because pool halls had bad reputations, her mother forbid Maria to go into the pool hall — she had to wait outside for the candy to be brought to her.[34]

• Tomomura Yushoshi, a physician, was respected for his honesty. Whenever a patient asked for information about his family background, Dr. Yushoshi replied honestly, "I am the son of a Nagasaki prostitute."[35]

Christmas

• *Guardian* columnist Emine Saner still gets excited about Christmas because "[t]his is the only time of year I still remember what it feels like to be a child." For one thing, Christmas was the only time she could engage in wish fulfillment: "[Y]ou ask for something, you write it down, and you magically get it. This is easy when you believe that a pair of grey-and-pink roller skates will make your life complete and indeed they do (Christmas, 1988)." Unfortunately, adults don't get excited the way a child gets excited on Christmas Eve. Ms. Saner once asked the 96-year-old great-grandmother of a friend what, if anything, she got excited about. The 96-year-old replied, "Death."[36]

• TV and radio talk-show host Joe Franklin made an effort never to get cocky about his success. He realized that his success was due to the cameras and the microphones, and if those ever went away, he would be nothing. He knew an influential newspaper columnist named Louis Sobol, who received 16,000 Christmas cards at the height of his power, influence, and fame. Unfortunately, his newspaper — the *Journal-American* — went out of business the following year and his column disappeared with it, and that Christmas he received only four Christmas cards — all of them from his relatives.[37]

Clothing

• For much of his career as a movie critic, Roger Ebert had a weight problem — he had too much of it. Once, he visited Sir John Soane's Museum at 13 Lincoln's Inn Fields, a museum that is known as "the most eccentric house in London." Sir John was a collector, and he collected books, brass buttons, coins, drawings, etchings, furniture, mirrors, oils, pistols, rifles, rugs, statuary, swords, tapestries, stuffed heads, watercolors, and writing implements. When Sir John, a great 18th-century architect, left his home to England, his wife said, "Now let them dust the bloody man's collection." In Sir John's breakfast room, Mr. Ebert saw a 17th-century chair, which was handsome and behind which (on the wall) was a card that said, "Have a seat on me!" Mr. Ebert prepared to take a seat, but a museum guard told him, "Oh, no, no, no, no, no, sir!" Mr. Ebert protested, "But it says to have a seat!" The guard replied, eying Mr. Ebert's sizable figure, "And so it does. But it's not for the likes of you!" In addition, Mr. Ebert once visited Bangkok, Thailand, where he saw a tailor shop with this sign in a window: "Fine Linen Summer Suit Made to Measure — $80." He went inside to inquire whether the sign were correct, and the proprietor looked at Mr. Ebert's sizable figure and said, "Well ... it 80 dollars suit, sure enough. But you — hundred dollar man." Mr. Ebert says, "It was a great deal.

For $100, I got a handsome white linen suit that fit me, and a story I could tell every time I wore it."[38]

• Sokai was a Zen monk whose clothing consisted of only one robe. One day, he washed the robe, then sat stark naked in a cemetery to wait for the robe to dry. A nobleman came to visit a grave and was astonished to see a naked Zen monk in the cemetery. Once Sokai had truthfully explained what he was doing, the nobleman bought him another robe. Eventually, Sokai became a Zen teacher, and the nobleman became one of his disciples.[39]

• Dame Marie Tempest wore clothes well, and she always looked good on stage. When she was dressed for a role, she always stood and never sat in her dressing room so that the costume stayed fresh. Once, an actress who was often late for work flung herself down before Dame Marie to ask for forgiveness, but Dame Marie ordered her, "Get up! Get up! Have you no respect for your management's clothes?"[40]

• On a very hot New York summer day, George S. Kaufman, Charles MacArthur, and Ben Hecht attended a meeting with powerful Broadway producer Jed Harris, who was stark naked in his office because of the heat. (This was before air conditioning.) As they were leaving after the meeting, Mr. Kaufman told Jed Harris, "Your fly is open."[41]

• At President George Washington's inauguration, the world was watching what the President would do, as his actions would say something about the new republic that had been created. Instead of appearing at his inauguration wearing silks and velvets, as a king would, President Washington wore the simple cloth known as homespun.[42]

• Lina Beacon, born 1898, remembered when the bra was invented. Her reaction: "I'm not wearing that thing!"[43]

Comedians

• Sam Levenson was a stand-up comedian who appeared several times on *The Ed Sullivan Show*, but a joke at a dinner that Mr. Sullivan chaired nearly ruined his TV career. After Mr. Sullivan's introduction of him at the diner, Mr. Levenson said, "Thank you, ladies and gentlemen. Thank you, Mr. Sullivan. There is an old legend that says that just before a child is born the angels kiss him and, says the legend, that on whatever part of him the angels kiss him will determine his particular talent on earth. If they kiss him on the head he will be an intellect; on the mouth an orator; on the hands an artisan, maybe a pianist. No one can prove exactly where Mr. Sullivan got kissed, but he sure makes a helluva chairman." The audience liked the joke, but Mr. Sullivan did not. It was a year before Mr. Levenson appeared on his show again.[44]

• Artie Stander was a radio and TV comedy writer of unparalleled chutzpah. A short man, he once said, "I could have been tall, but I turned it down." Once, Mr. Stander was writing with Charlie Isaacs. Mr. Isaacs used to pace the floor and occasionally jump up and touch the ceiling with his fingertips. Mr. Stander watched him for a while, then said, "I can do that." Short as he was, he attempted to jump up and touch the ceiling several times, failing each time, then finally gave it up, putting the blame for his failure on his habit of smoking cigarettes. Another time, his wife saw him standing on the seat of the toilet, peeing down into the bowl. He explained, "I just wanted to see what it felt like to be [the very tall] Gary Cooper."[45]

• TV and radio talk-show host Joe Franklin interviewed many, many celebrities, often before they became truly famous. Unfortunately, many of the celebrities, once they became truly famous, did not appear again on his show. One exception was Bill Cosby. In 1993, when Mr. Cosby was a superstar, he appeared on Mr. Franklin's show, astounding his press people, who wondered why he didn't go on a national show instead. Mr. Cosby explained, "I don't want to forget the man who gave me my first break, when I didn't have carfare to come to the studio."[46]

• Comedian Bob Newhart used to watch other comedians on *The Ed Sullivan Show* and rate their performances to see if he still owned the title of the funniest man in America. Usually, he would say to himself after watching a new comedian, "Well, fella, you're okay, but not socko. We still know who's number one." But one evening he watched a new comedian by the name of Bill Cosby. This time, he said, "Good luck, kid. Take it and run with it for a while."[47]

• Comedian Jack Carter was compulsive about certain things. For example, he dusted frequently and runs the vacuum, making sure his house is clean. In addition, he checked to see what kind of china he was eating from whenever he ate in a restaurant or at a friend's. Once, he was Lucille Ball's guest. Lucy knew of his compulsion, so when Mr. Carter lifted the plate to look at its bottom and see what kind it was, he found a note from Lucy: "You schmuck, it's Wedgewood."[48]

• Comedian Red Skelton did anything for a laugh. At the Brown Derby restaurant, he once took off his necktie, cut it into little pieces, put it in his Caesar salad, and ate it. By the way, Universal Studios once called all its stars together for an end-of-the-year photograph. Mr. Skelton arrived late. Instead of apologizing, he stood on a chair, and announced to the stars, "You can all go home now — the part's been casted."[49]

• Bob Hope was disappointed with his first comedy short, "Going Spanish." When columnist Walter Winchell asked him about the movie, Mr. Hope replied, "When they catch John Dillinger, they're going to make him sit through it twice." Mr. Winchell printed the joke in his column; unfortunately, the producers of the comedy short didn't like the joke, so they fired Mr. Hope.[50]

• Art Linkletter occasionally entertained in military hospitals where his audience consisted of soldiers with multiple amputations. Because he knew that the soldiers didn't want sympathy, he would sometimes joke to people who had no arms, "Well, you guys aren't going to be much of a help with the applause."[51]

Chapter 2: From Crime and Justice to Gays and Lesbians

Crime and Justice

• What will result in justice: for two disputants to go into a court of law with lawyers representing each side, or for two disputants to go before a rabbi? To answer this question, Rabbi Avraham Yehoshua told this story: A wolf once killed a deer, but before it could eat the deer, a lion came along and took the deer from the wolf. Seeking justice, the wolf asked a fox to judge the dispute. The wolf claimed that he deserved the deer because he had killed it, but the lion claimed that he deserved the deer because he was the king of the jungle. The fox said that the only reasonable solution was to divide the deer, giving the wolf and the lion an equal share. However, when the fox divided the deer, it was not in equal halves, so the fox took a big bite of the larger half. Now the other half was bigger than the first half, so the fox took a big bite out of it, making the first half bigger than the second half. This continued until the fox had eaten the deer, leaving only bones for the wolf and the lion. A court of law is often like the fox: By the time the lawsuit is settled and the lawyers have received their payment, nothing is left for the disputants.[52]

• Some of the parties held by Divine, an actress who appeared in many of John Waters' films, were remarkable. At one party, she auctioned off all of her landlady's furniture in the furnished apartment. Divine once hosted a fabulous party at the Hilton. Everything was so luxurious that the Hilton asked for permission to take photographs for their brochures. Divine readily gave permission, but unfortunately her guests kept covering their faces when someone tried to take a photograph of them — nearly all of Divine's guests were either wanted by the police, or on parole, or in trouble in other ways.[53]

• Wilson Mizner and Sammy Finn left the Brown Derby one foggy night, when they noticed that they were being followed by two men who apparently intended to rob them. Mr. Wilson said to Mr. Finn, "You take the big guy, and I'll take the little guy with the knife." Fortunately, they got away from the two men in the foggy night, and it wasn't until later that Mr. Finn realized that the fog had been so thick that it was impossible for Mr. Mizner to see whether the little guy had had a knife.[54]

Critics

• Thomas Beecham once used a tenor with an Italian name in some of his concerts. After the first concert, the critics commented on the tenor's pronunciation of the various languages in which he had sung. The critics believed that the tenor had sung well in his native Italian and was adequate in French, but that his German was horrible. After reading what the critics had said, Mr. Beecham discovered that the tenor was actually German, but had taken an Italian name for professional purposes.[55]

• When the future Sir Rudolf Bing was growing up, his family sometimes held musical evenings in which live music was played. At one such evening, the Rothschild Quartet played music by Egon Wellesz. Because the chairs were too short for the musicians, they placed some volumes of Schubert chamber music on the seat of the chairs, then sat down. Sir Rudolf remembers wishing that they had sat on the music of Wellesz and had played the music of Schubert.[56]

• Lesbian cartoonist Alison Bechdel's comic strip, *Dykes to Watch Out For*, contains feminists of all kinds: white, black, Asian, Latina, handicapped, able-bodied, thin, fat, butch, femme. *Publisher's Weekly* once said about *Dykes to Watch Out For* that it is "politically correct and racially diverse to a fault." However, Ms. Bechdel isn't bothered by such criticism, if in fact it is criticism.[57]

Death

• Andy Warhol occasionally used an impersonator, Alan Midgette, to stand in for him when he didn't feel like giving a lecture. After Andy died, Mr. Midgette would occasionally impersonate him at parties. Andy's friends, who of course knew that Andy was dead, would tell Mr. Midgette, "Oh, Andy, we're so glad you're back." Chances are, Andy would have approved. He hated to admit that someone he liked had died; instead, he would say that they had gone shopping. And after his mother died, if anyone asked him how she was, he would say that she was fine but didn't get out much.[58]

• Ludwig van Beethoven was a true original. He had a terrible temper, and he once dumped a dish of veal and gravy over a waiter's head. In his old age, Beethoven was hard on pianos. As he grew deafer, he pounded on the piano keys harder, trying to hear the piano and breaking its strings. And according to Anselm Hüttenbrenner, as Beethoven lay dying in 1827, a storm arose. Beethoven came out of his coma and shook his fist at the heavens. Following a flash of lightning and a clap of thunder, he died.[59]

• Sheldon Leonard made his first movie in Jamaica, where he was advised to dispose of his nail clippings so that they could not be used to make a voodoo doll and put a curse on him. At a party near Kingston, the host was a dead man who was propped up by a table laden with fruits and meats. The corpse was not buried until it had decomposed so much that it would be useless as a zombie.[60]

• Hector Gray visited his friend, ventriloquist Ray Scott, who was dying of throat cancer, on his deathbed. After the visit, Mr. Gray said, "Good night. I'll see you tomorrow." Mr. Scott replied, "Perhaps you will, but I won't be seeing you." Mr. Scott was right — he died during the night.[61]

• Samuel Baldwin's wife promised to dance on his grave when he died. That's why, when Mr. Baldwin did die, in 1736, his will made provisions for his burial at sea.[62]

• When Rumi died, with his last words he asked that he be buried in the topmost part of his tomb, as he wanted to be the first to rise on resurrection day.[63]

Easter

• Country comedian Jerry Clower is a devout Christian who attends Baptist church each Sunday, and sometimes he gets a little upset at Christians who attend church only on Easter. Once, while driving to Easter services, he told his wife, Homerline, "Darling, if there's a lost man sitting in the pew where I usually sit this morning, on Easter Sunday, I'll kneel by him and pray or stand outside in the rain. He can have my seat. But if a Baptist is in my seat that ain't been there since last Easter, he's getting up."[64]

Education

• Teachers, of course, sometimes run into difficulties, often of a funny nature: 1) One teacher used to help herself remember which child went with each name by writing a short description of a child by his or her name. This led to a problem: A boy saw the description "Looks like Woody Allen" by his name, and he told his parents, who were not happy about the description. 2) A teacher disciplined a child who told him that his name was Daniel Stephens. After she had given a few detentions to "Daniel Stephens," the real Daniel Stephens came to her and asked why she was punishing him with detentions. 3) A teacher forgot to pack her lunch and was forced to buy and eat an egg sandwich, which filled her with gas. After she broke wind very loudly in front of her students, they gave her unflattering nicknames for a few weeks. 4) A student teacher muttered "Actually" under his breath, but what the teacher observing him thought he had muttered was "Oh, sh*t," a phrase the observing teacher wrote about on the evaluation of his teaching performance.[65]

• Helen Lieberstein Shaphren taught deaf children, and she took the children each week to an ice cream parlor, where they ordered a cone of whatever flavor ice cream they wanted; however, if they did not speak clearly enough for the proprietor of the ice cream parlor to understand them, they got vanilla ice cream. One boy cried when he got vanilla ice cream instead of the chocolate ice cream he wanted, but Ms. Shaphren remained firm. It took months of effort for the little boy to order clearly enough for the proprietor of the ice cream parlor to understand his order, but when he did, both Mrs. Shaphren and the proprietor of the ice cream parlor cried. (Mrs. Shaphren was a pioneer of education for deaf children. She once applied for a teaching job and was told that Arizona had no need of special education but she could teach in a regular classroom. She declined the job offer, and she opened a school for deaf children in her home.)[66]

• Russell Johnson, who played the Professor on *Gilligan's Island*, had the hardest lines to learn because so much of what he said was explaining how he was able to use science to do such things as recharge batteries with nothing more than seawater and various metals. Bob Denver, who played Gilligan, once asked Mr. Johnson how he was able to learn his lines. The explanation was simple, although the work involved was not. Mr. Johnson spent hours reading the encyclopedia so he could understand what he was saying. The hours of reading paid off — he seldom blew his lines. (But on the rare occasions he did, his fellow castmembers were ready to tease him by saying such things as "Gee, Russ, can't you learn the stupid lines!")[67]

• George Balanchine was even tempered, but he could and did criticize dancers. Sometimes, he would tell a dancer, "Don't you know what fifth position is, dear? Didn't anyone ever tell you? Where did you study?" (The dancer had studied at his own School of American Ballet.) Dancer Merrill Ashley says about Mr. Balanchine's criticism that "with that question, he had made his point, with devastating effect." Although Mr. Balanchine was a strict dance teacher, he was a well-loved dance teacher. After his classes ended, the students often briefly but appreciatively applauded — something he was unable to stop the students from doing.[68]

• M.E. Kerr, who became the author of *Dinky Hocker Shoots Smack!*, and her parents disagreed about where she should go to college. She wanted to go to the University of Missouri, and her parents wanted her to stay close to home and go to Syracuse University. As it turned out, her grades were so poor that neither school accepted her. She ended up attending Vermont Junior College, which was a good choice for her. She started the school newspaper, and she got good training for being an author by writing most of the newspaper's articles.[69]

• As a child, American artist Sam Gilliam's favorite thing to draw on was the cardboard that came with laundered shirts. Fortunately, a laundry was located down the street from where he lived, so he had a ready supply of his favorite drawing material. His fifth-grade class used to hold contests for the best student-created works of art, and Sam won so often that his teacher said, "You know, you ought to be an artist." Young Sam thought for a second, then said, "I think I will."[70]

• A 7th-grade student in Olympia, Washington, broke lots and lots of rules, including tripping every student who walked past his desk and shooting spit balls at innocent students. One day, his teacher kept him after class because he had snapped a ballpoint pen, getting ink everywhere. She worked him very hard, making him do chore after chore until he said something that made her smile: "Oh, fairy Godmother, where are you?"[71]

• When Steve Wynn was asked what was the best piece of advice he has actually followed, he told a jazz anecdote about John Coltrane saying to Miles Davis, "Man, when I'm going on a solo sometimes I just don't know how to stop." Mr. Davis replied, "Maybe you should take the horn out of your mouth." This reply is wise, and Mr. Wynn says, "I always try to know when it's time to take the horn out of my mouth."[72]

• Violinist Josef Gingold once found himself in an elevator with an elderly Arturo Toscanini, who was carrying and studying the score of Beethoven's *Eroica*, which he would rehearse that day. Mr. Toscanini told Mr. Gingold, "*Caro*, I've studied 55 years this symphony, but is always possible, eh, that I could forget about one *sforzando*."[73]

• The Sufi poet Rumi once started to give a lecture near a marsh, but the croaking of the frogs in the lake drowned out his voice. Therefore, Rumi spoke to the frogs in the marsh, saying, "What is all this noise about? Either be quiet, or give a lecture." The frogs became silent, and they stayed silent until Rumi gave them permission to croak again.[74]

Fans

• Alan Hale played the Skipper for three years on *Gilligan's Island*, and for the rest of his life, he wore a Skipper's hat and of course was constantly recognized. In a restaurant, he was recognized immediately, so he asked his waitress to head off any fans wanting him to sign autographs until after he had eaten, when he would be happy to speak to fans. The waitress did as she had been requested, and after Mr. Hale had eaten, she requested an autograph for herself, saying, "Captain Kangaroo, you were one of my favorites." Mr. Hale signed the autograph, "All the best, Capt. Kangaroo."[75]

• Carol Klein was a young superfan who followed a singing group called the Tokens all over Brooklyn. Wherever the Tokens were performing, young Carol was sure to be there. Tokens member Neil Sedaka even wrote a song titled "Oh! Carol" and dedicated it to her. Years later, Carol Klein had become singer/songwriter Carole King, and she wrote a song titled "Oh! Neil" and dedicated it to him.[76]

• Woody Allen has noticed something interesting about autograph seekers. It just takes one courageous autograph seeker to set off a wave of autograph seekers. In a restaurant without courageous autograph seekers, Mr. Allen can eat in peace although 50 people may recognize him, but if just one person asks him for an autograph, the other 49 people will also ask him for an autograph.[77]

• An admirer once said to James Abbott McNeill Whistler that the world had only two real painters: Whistler and Diego Velasquez. Mr. Whistler replied, "Why drag in Velasquez?"[78]

Fights

• Martial artists are loathe to fight real combats, believing that the very best way to win a fight is to avoid fighting at all. Gichin Funakoshi, an Okinawan schoolteacher who revived the art of karate in modern times, believed, "To win 100 victories in 100 battles is not the highest skill. To subdue the enemy without fighting is the highest skill." Sometimes, people would challenge Mr. Funakoshi to fight in an attempt to prove how tough they were, but he always walked away from these fights. Once, he explained why: "When two tigers fight, one is always injured. The other is dead."[79]

• In 1957, New York Yankee Billy Martin had a birthday party that turned into a fight at the Copacabana. Hank Bauer was arrested, and some other Yankees got their names in the newspaper, revealing that they had broken training. Angry, manager Casey Stengel quickly took action, benching most of the players involved, but not benching hitter Mickey Mantle, who had also been involved at the Copacabana. Asked about the discrepancy, Mr. Stengel said, "I may be mad, but I'm not mad enough to lose the pennant."[80]

Food

• The Jai Lai in Columbus, Ohio, was Ohio State University football coach Woody Hayes' favorite restaurant. He ate there alone, with his family, and with recruits and their families. One day, when Woody was eating alone, Jai Lai co-owner Dave Girves was approached by a kid who asked him, "Do you think it'll make the coach mad if I interrupt his dinner to ask for an autograph?" Mr. Girves answered, "No," correctly. Coach Hayes ended up talking to the kid for over two hours. On another occasion, Coach Hayes ordered take-out, not for himself, but for a relative who loved seafood but who was in a hospital where she hated the food. Mr. Girves told Coach Hayes that the meal was free, that Coach Hayes had always paid for all of his meals, and that the restaurant wanted to give the seafood dinner to his relative. Coach Hayes would not allow the restaurant to do that. He threatened, "If you don't let me pay for the meal, I'll never be back." Mr. Girves knew that Coach Hayes was serious, so he let him pay for the meal.[81]

• Folger's once made a famous series of TV commercials in which its representatives supposedly went into fancy restaurants and replaced the brewed coffee with Folger's instant coffee. Of course, the actors playing the customers didn't notice the difference. Regina, a company that manufactured vacuum cleaners, made fun of those commercials in its own commercials. Its representatives (actually, actors) supposedly went into fancy restaurants and replaced the brewed coffee with sand and ground-up clam shells. Of course, the actors playing the customers choked and spit the "coffee" on the floor, which was promptly and efficiently cleaned with a Regina vacuum cleaner.[82]

• James McNeill Whistler, the famous painter, attended West Point, where he performed very badly. He once outraged an examiner who was shocked that Mr. Whistler did not know the date of the Battle of Buena Vista. The examiner asked, "Suppose you were to go out to dinner, and the company began to talk of the Mexican war, and you, a West Point man, were asked the date of the battle, what would you do?" Mr. Whistler replied, "Do? Why, I should refuse to associate with people who could talk of such things at dinner."[83]

• The producers of the 1980s TV series *Family Ties* had a hard time convincing NBC executive Brandon Tartikoff that Michael J. Fox was a good choice to star as Alex P. Keaton, the greedy Republican kid. Mr. Tartikoff argued, "The kid's good, but can you see his face on a lunchbox?" *Family Ties*, of course, became a huge hit, as did Mr. Fox' *Back to the Future* movies. The producers of *Family Ties* eventually gave a Michael J. Fox lunchbox to Mr. Tartikoff, along with a note: "Dear Brandon, this is for you to put your crow in."[84]

• The father of M.E. Kerr, author of books for young adults, manufactured mayonnaise for a living until World War II started in 1939. Mayonnaise was not an essential food, so instead of making mayonnaise, he began to make dehydrated onions. Because of this, the entire town of Auburn, New York, smelled like onions. Therefore, her father placed this ad in the local newspaper, "Our onions are for field rations for our fighting men. When you smell onions, pray for peace."[85]

• Comedian Jackie Gleason, of course, was a big eater. Early in his career, he and a friend named Tony Amico stopped at a vegetarian restaurant called the Ideal Restaurant. They weren't vegetarians, but they decided to eat there because of this sign: "All you can eat for fifty-five cents." Each of them ate triple servings of every vegetable in the restaurant's menu, and when they left, the owner took down the sign that had attracted the two big eaters.[86]

• Igor Youskevitch, who danced in a famous partnership with Alicia Alonso, once got in trouble with the tax collectors. He danced hard, and needing to refresh his body, he ate two steak dinners a day. Naturally, he regarded the steak dinners as legitimate business expenses for a hard-working dancer, but the tax collector did not agree and advised him, "Eat in cheaper restaurants."[87]

• Poet James Stephens was worried about the prospect of attending a formal dinner party, at which he would have women seated on either side of him, so he asked George Moore for advice. Mr. Moore replied, "Don't touch their knees. Women have an instinctive knowledge whether a man who touches her knee is caressing her or only wiping his greasy fingers on her stockings."[88]

• In the movie *Quo Vadis?* the character played by former heavyweight champion Buddy Baer killed a bull with his bare hands. The next day, his manager sent him a steak and the note, "From the bull you killed." Mr. Baer sent back the steak and another note, "I refuse to eat a fellow actor."[89]

Free Speech

• Jennifer Camper, a lesbian, once drew a controversial cartoon titled "Naughty Things to Do with Communion Wafers." The genesis of the cartoon lay in public comment about a 1989 protest by AIDS activists inside New York's St. Patrick's Cathedral. During the protest, some communion wafers fell on the floor, and public comment centered on the communion wafers and the supposed insult to Catholicism. Ms. Camper drew the cartoon because of her outrage that people were more upset over the communion wafers than over the many thousands of deaths due to AIDS.[90]

• Back when Tipper Gore was trying to have legislation passed that would require mandatory labels on media such as records, comedian Bill Hicks had this label (that quoted Thomas Jefferson) put on one of his albums: "Are we to have a censor whose imprimatur shall say what books may be sold and what we may buy?" On another album, he put this label: "This album contains everything your parents hate, everything the church preaches against, and everything the government fears. Enjoy."[91]

Gambling

• While in London, Chico and Harpo Marx ran across an expatriate American comedian who cheated at cards by using a marked deck (something they found out after losing a couple of weeks' salary to him at the poker table), so they decided to teach him a lesson. First, they asked that the game be changed to auction pinochle the next time they played. The actor was willing to change, since marked cards are a marked advantage in any card game. Then they set up a game at the actor's apartment. Next, to get ready for the game, Chico and Harpo set up a system of signals so that *they* could cheat. Finally, they brought some new packs of unopened (and unmarked) cards along with them. At the actor's apartment, Chico and Harpo proceeded to win the actor's money. The night grew dark, the fireplace burned all the available firewood, and Chico and Harpo grew cold and ready to leave. However, the actor wanted a chance to win his money back, so he started to burn his furniture in the fireplace to keep Chico and Harpo warm enough to play cards. Early the next morning, all of the furniture, including the chairs and the table they had been playing cards on, had been burned up, Chico and Harpo were freezing, and they departed — taking with them $6,000 of the actor's money. Chico and Harpo hailed a taxicab, and they ordered the cabbie to drive them to the warmest restaurant in London. This puzzled the cabbie, who asked, "Don't you mean the best restaurant in London?" Harpo replied, "We don't care if it's good or not. Just get us where it's warm. After our blood starts circulating again, we'll decide where to eat."[92]

• Chico and Harpo, two of the famous Marx Brothers, were almost equal in height, but Chico was 1/16 of an inch taller. Occasionally, they would bet $5 on who was taller, with the taller person getting the money, and Harpo always lost. But one day Harpo said, "Fifty dollars says that I'm taller." Chico bet the money, and Harpo was just over an inch taller, even after both brothers had taken off their shoes. Chico paid the money, and he learned later that Harpo had gone to a place that advertised, "Increase your height dramatically!" For several hours, he had been stretched, and for several hours, he was an inch taller, then he returned to his normal height.[93]

• A man and his wife went to Las Vegas for a vacation. While the husband was taking a shower, the wife went into the casino to play roulette. She put $2 on number 17 and won. In fact, she let the money ride and kept winning — number 17 came up 17 times in a row on the wheel she was playing and turned her $2 into $50,000. Unfortunately, she continued to let the money ride and played number 17 one more time, but a different number came up and she lost all the money. She went back to her hotel room, where her husband asked her, "How'd you do?" She replied, "I lost $2."[94]

• Lord Brampton, formerly Mr. Hawkins, was a judge who enjoyed gambling on the races. One day a member of the jury had a telegram put into his hand. Reading the telegram, he was overjoyed, and shouted, "Silvio's won, and I've won." Judge Hawkins criticized the outburst severely, saying, "It is most improper, and I trust it will never occur again." Then Judge Hawkins asked, "By the way, did the telegram say what was second and third?"[95]

• Frank Sullivan enjoyed betting on the horse races, and he was honored once by the New York Racing Association with the one-time-only running of the Frank Sullivan Purse. On such a wonderful day, Mr. Sullivan wanted to be sure he had the winning ticket — so he bet on every horse in the race.[96]

Gays and Lesbians

• According to rumor, gay actor Ernest Thesiger always wore a string of pearls around his neck. At the beginning of World War II, while he was in Oxford, the air raid siren went off, and he went to an air raid shelter where he attracted a lot of attention because of his clothing — Russian high-necked pajamas and a truly spectacular dressing gown — and because he was busily engaging in his hobby of needlework. Soon, the other people in the shelter began to sleep and Mr. Thesiger knew that he wasn't attracting as much attention as before — so he grabbed his throat and shouted, "My God! My pearls! No, no, it's all right. I've got them on."[97]

• In September 2009, same-sex marriage became legal in Vermont. To celebrate, Ben & Jerry's, the famed ice-cream company, temporarily renamed its Chubby Hubby ice cream Hubby Hubby ice cream. Response to the move was positive. Sean Greenwood, Ben & Jerry's grand pooh-bah of public relations (I did not make that up — it is his real title) received an email from a lesbian in Illinois, where same-sex marriage is not legal. In the email the woman said that she cried when she heard her daughter say, "At least Ben & Jerry's recognizes mommy and mommy are married."[98]

Chapter 3: From Good Deeds to Money

Good Deeds

• Animals can be heroes — how cool is that? In 2001, nine-year-old Pam was pushing her sleeping Siamese cat, Sybil, in a baby carriage near her home in a suburb of Detroit, Michigan. A stranger got out of an automobile, covered Pam's mouth with tape, and tried to force her into the car. She grabbed Sybil out of the baby carriage, and now awake, Sybil clawed the man's arm and then jumped up on his chest and bit his throat. He managed to throw the cat on the ground, but by then he was surrounded with adults from the neighborhood, who were armed with bats, golf clubs, and even canes. The police came quickly and arrested the man.[99]

• Phyllis Bickerstaff has a son named Jefferson who suffered brain damage at birth, resulting in impaired motor skills. Jefferson has a dog named Jett. One of the things that Jett does is to help Jefferson overcome the stigma of having a disability. When Jefferson is with Jett, people can see that the two love each other. Children are fascinated by Jett's shaking hands and retrieving things, and so they don't focus on the fact that Jefferson has to crawl on his hands and knees instead of walking. Jefferson and Jett attend Boy Scout meetings together.[100]

• Newspapers — even rival newspapers — sometimes do favors for each other. A fire at the *Chicago Times* meant that it was unable to print off copies of its latest edition, so it used — with permission — the press of the rival newspaper *Chicago Tribune*. The headline for the *Times'* story about the event said, "Hot Off the Press (The *Tribune's*)."[101]

Halloween

• *Guardian* columnist Hadley Freeman remembers the excellent Halloween costumes that her sister wore at ages seven and eight. Once she went as a grand piano — she wore black tights and a black leotard and gold pumps, and she hung a paper keyboard around her neck. Another year she went as a bag of jellybeans — she cut out two holes for her feet in a large clear trash bag and filled it with balloons of various colors.[102]

Husbands and Wives

• A married couple was having difficulties in their marriage, and so the husband consulted a lawyer to arrange for a divorce. The lawyer agreed to put together the necessary papers for the divorce within a month's time, but he told the husband that the man's wife would be very upset because of the divorce. Therefore, to cut down on the wife's pain, the lawyer made the husband promise to buy his wife a gift every day and to compliment her every day. A month later, the husband stopped by the lawyer's office to say that he wouldn't need a divorce now because he and his wife were getting along a lot better. He also asked the lawyer how much he owed him for putting together the divorce papers. "Don't worry about it," the lawyer said. "I've been busy, so I didn't have time to put them together. Besides, I had the feeling that if you followed my advice you wouldn't need them."[103]

• Pioneer preacher Lorenzo Dow had a loving wife, Peggy, who unfortunately died young. Wanting to get married again, Mr. Dow went to an evening meeting and afterward announced that he would marry whichever woman stood up next. Two women immediately jumped to their feet, and Mr. Dow chose the woman who was the quickest to jump up. Unfortunately, she was a shrew who was completely unlike his first wife, and their marriage was unhappy. After his marriage, Mr. Dow saw a sign that an unhappily married male neighbor had put up on his property: "Women Rule Here." He then went to his own property and put up his own sign: "Here, Too."[104]

• Thomas Dolby, who is probably most famous for his song "She Blinded Me With Science," found it easy to give up smoking at age 28. He met actress Kathleen Beller, and she told him that if he smoked, she would never kiss him. Mr. Dolby says, "I really wanted to kiss her. So that did the trick." They married and had children.[105]

• Author Peg Bracken recommends that husbands and wives work out a set of code words. For example, if the wife usually calls her husband "Dear," but at a party she suddenly calls him "Sweetie," that may mean she is telling him in code, "I'm tired and want to go home — get me out of here."[106]

Illnesses and Injuries

• Maria was a 10-year-old Mexican girl who was badly hurt in a car accident and went into and stayed in a coma. At home, she stayed in the coma for seven months. Fortunately, on July 27, 1976, a stray cat came in through an open window and started licking Maria's thumb. Maria's fingers twitched — this was the most movement that Maria had made on her own since going into the coma. Maria's mother prayed, *Wake, up, Maria. Wake up, Maria.* The cat stayed in Maria's bedroom and kept licking her hand. On the eighth day after the cat had started licking her hand, Maria woke up. She recovered rapidly.[107]

• Health care has changed since the good old days. Annie Cogburn, born 1893, remembered when a doctor would come to the rural area in North Carolina she grew up in to see someone who was really sick. People used to stand by the side of the road and flag down the doctor's car, and then tell him their symptoms. The doctor would listen, and then give them a pill. According to Ms. Cogburn, "He just gave everyone the same pill. And they would get better. Just so they got a pill from the doctor, they were happy."[108]

• In the 1800s, mothers with crying infants could quiet them by giving them such medicines as Mother Bailey's Quieting Syrup or Mrs. Winslow's Soothing Syrup. These medicines were very effective in quieting infants — as they well should be, since the medicines contained a form of opium. Also in the 1800s, a very popular tonic for women was Lydia Pinkham's Vegetable Tonic for Female Problems. No wonder it was popular — it was 18 percent alcohol![109]

• British actor Stanley Holloway once suffered from a tremendous toothache that made his face swell up while he was on tour in South

Africa. He was in so much pain that his producer arranged for him to see a doctor and a dentist at the same time. The doctor gave him a shot in his rear end while the dentist worked on his bleeding mouth. The doctor then said to the dentist, "My end isn't bleeding."[110]

Insults

• A man made an appointment with Mulla Nasrudin, but Nasrudin forgot the appointment. Therefore, the man, who had called at Nasrudin's home but had been told that Nasrudin was not in, wrote "Stupid Idiot" on Nasrudin's door and then went home. When Nasrudin returned home and saw the graffito, he went to the man's house and said, "I had forgotten our appointment, and I am sorry that I was not at home. Of course, I remembered our appointment when I saw your name on my door."[111]

• During an election, a politician once grew angry at Parliament member Richard Brinsley Sheridan and said that he would knock his brains out. Mr. Sheridan stayed calm and said to the crowd of onlookers, "You have heard my opponent's amiable desire. I have but one suggestion to make. Let him be very careful when he performs the operation. Let him pick up my brains, for he needs them sadly."[112]

• In 1931, several Italian opera singers sailed to the Colon in Buenos Aires. Among the singers were baritone Titta Ruffo and tenor Galliano Masini. Perhaps expecting a compliment, Mr. Masini asked Mr. Ruffo, "After Caruso, who is the world's greatest tenor?" However, he did not receive a compliment. Instead, Mr. Ruffo replied, "One fart from Caruso would drown out all the tenors active today."[113]

• A member of The Players Club enjoyed talking often and at great length on many topics, including his favorite, which was his acquaintance with baseball pitcher Christy Mathewson. When Mr. Mathewson died, Tom Chalmers noted that it would cut the loquacious member's conversation by 50 percent. Franklin Pierce Adams snapped, "A drop in the bucket."[114]

• Dr. Samuel Johnson disliked Scotland. At a dinner party, his hostess served a Scottish dish, then asked how he liked it. Dr. Johnson said, "Madam, it is a dish fit only for pigs." His hostess replied, "Let me help you to more of it."[115]

• The great conqueror Tamburlaine grew annoyed at Mulla Nasrudin, who was seated a couple of yards from him. Tamburlaine said, "You are not far removed from a donkey, Nasrudin." Nasrudin replied, "No, only about six feet.[116]

Language

• Problems occurred at frontier religious camp meetings. For one thing, a different kind of camp would often be set up nearby — a camp where non-religious people could drink and gamble. Another problem occurred when people of a different religious denomination would crash some other religion's camp meeting. For example, Methodist circuit rider Peter Cartwright was once bothered at a camp meeting by a group of what he called Mormons. An elderly female Mormon began to talk and shout in an unknown tongue, so he told her to stop speaking gibberish. When she said (in English) that she had a message for him direct from God, he replied, "I will have none of your messages. If God can speak through no better medium than an old, hypocritical, lying woman, I will hear nothing of it." He then told the old woman (and all the Mormons), "This is my camp meeting, and I will maintain the good order of it. Don't show your face here again, nor one of the Mormons. If you do, you will get Lynch's Law." Confronted with that prospect, the Mormons quickly disappeared, and Mr. Cartwright carried on.[117]

• A Scotswoman was asked what she thought of the minister's sermon that morning. She replied, "How did he get on? Ah, he just stood there and threw stones at us, and never missed with any of them. Now that was preaching!"[118]

Letters

• When Rudolf Bing was working at the Städtische Opera, a problem occurred that involved Carl Ebert, manager; Fritz Stiedry, conductor; and Paul Breisach, another conductor. Mr. Ebert offered the job of conducting the opening-night *Macbeth* to Mr. Stiedry, but Mr. Stiedry turned it down, so Mr. Ebert offered the job to Mr. Breisach. As soon as Mr. Stiedry heard that Mr. Breisach had accepted the job, he changed his mind and wanted to conduct it. Since Mr. Stiedry had been his original choice, Mr. Ebert decided to let him conduct *Macbeth*. Therefore, he turned to Mr. Bing, who was a cousin and friend to Mr. Breisach, and asked him to compose a nice letter to Mr. Breisach, letting him down easy, but saying that Mr. Stiedry was going to conduct *Macbeth*. After Mr. Bing had written the letter, Mr. Ebert signed it and mailed it. When Mr. Breisach received the letter, he went to Mr. Bing and asked him to compose a letter to Mr. Ebert, saying that he still wanted to conduct *Macbeth* as he had been asked to do. Mr. Bing writes in his autobiography, *5000 Nights at the Opera*, "For some time I was engaged in a delicate correspondence with myself!" Eventually, Mr. Breisach accepted Mr. Stiedry's conducting of *Macbeth*.[119]

• Groucho Marx' son is Arthur, who gave Groucho two grandsons: Steve and Andy. When Steve was eight years old, Arthur and his wife, Irene, discovered a new item among Steve's collection of items: a wallet-sized reproduction of Marilyn Monroe's nude calendar photograph. They asked Steve where he had found it, and he replied, "A vacant lot." They noticed that the photo had been torn and repaired with tape, so they asked Steve how the photo had gotten torn. He replied, "Andy [his younger brother] tried to take it away from me." Eventually, they discovered that the photo actually belonged to Grandpa Groucho, and so Steve wrote a letter of apology to Groucho for taking the photograph and put the letter in an envelope along with the photo and $1 — his idea, and a generous one, as $1 represented 10 weeks of his allowance all those many decades ago. The letter amused

Groucho, and he gave the $1 to Arthur, telling him to return it to Steve. He also gave the photo of the nude Marilyn Monroe to Arthur, telling him to give it to Steve as well because "I'm getting too old for that sort of thing."[120]

• Tom Wolfe's first magazine article was supposed to be about car customizers in Los Angeles, but he discovered that he lacked the confidence to write a magazine article. Therefore, he wrote a memo to Byron Dobell, editor of *Esquire*, in which he wrote down all of the notes he had taken, hoping that another writer could do the article using his notes. He says, "It became very much like a letter that you would write to a friend in which you're not thinking about style, you're just pouring it all out, and I churned it out all night long, forty typewritten, triple-spaced pages." Fortunately, Bryon liked what he read, and he called Tom to say, "We're knocking the 'Dear Byron' off the top of your memo, and we're running the piece."[121]

• During the first season of *Gilligan's Island*, Russell Johnson and Dawn Wells weren't mentioned in the TV series' theme song — they were merely referred to as "the rest." After the series was over, Mr. Johnson and Ms. Wells remained friends, and Ms. Wells signs her letters and cards to him with "Love, the rest."[122]

• An English schoolboy once wrote his parents: "S.O.S. L.S.D. R.S.V.P." (By the way, the initials of "L.S.D." are the abbreviations of English money — pounds, shillings, and pence.)[123]

Media

• Long ago, reporters sometimes resorted to thievery in order to get a good story. For example, a reporter who did NOT work for the *Chicago Tribune* heard that a man named something like John Jones had been murdered. He got a policeman's star from his editor and went to Mr. Jones' apartment building, where he flashed his star at the apartment building superintendent and asked to be let inside Mr. Jones' apartment, which he ransacked for letters and a diary, which he carried to his car. Just then, Mr. Jones arrived, safe and sound. The reporter told him, "Jones, you have caused us a great deal of trouble. Now hop upstairs and phone the detective bureau. Tell 'em to take you off the death list. Of course, the reporter didn't need the letters and diary anymore. Therefore, he went to the building that housed the rival *Tribune*. He hailed a cab and paid the driver to deliver a package containing the letter and diary to Mr. Jones, along with a message saying that the package was from the *Tribune*. Soon Mr. Jones was calling the *Tribune* and threatening to sue the newspaper for invasion of privacy and for illegal entry.[124]

• After a few months of not attending classes, controversial filmmaker John Waters was thrown out of New York University because he smoked marijuana. He was told not to tell anyone why he was expelled, his parents were called to come and get him, and guards were placed outside of his room so he couldn't escape before his parents got him. To get revenge on NYU and embarrass the university, Mr. Waters picked up the telephone in his room and called the newspapers to tell them about the drug scandal at NYU. Big headlines appeared in major newspapers the following day, and the scandal was even written up in Richard Goldstein's book *Drugs on Campus*.[125]

• In 1848, the Pittsburgh *Daily Gazette* published an article about a young woman who wanted to commit suicide by throwing herself into a local canal and drowning, but when she reached the canal, it stank horribly, and so she decided to postpone committing suicide until she reached cleaner water.[126]

Mishaps

• For about 10 years, Roger Ebert lived in an attic apartment at 2437 N. Burling, finally moving after buying a coach house. Mr. Ebert loved the attic apartment, which he regarded as perfect and which he rented from Paul and Anna Dudak, whom he loved. When he moved, he had a house-warming party, which was attended by his friends Sherman Wolf and John McHugh, among others. At the party, Mr. Wolf told him, "Congratulations on your new house! You've worked hard and you deserve it. It's a real step up from that pig-pen you used to live in." Mr. Ebert replied, "Sherman, I don't believe you've met my landlady from Burling Street, Mrs. Dudak." Embarrassed, Mr. Wolf turned red and said, "Oh, my God! Oh, Mrs. Dudak, actually it was a very nice place, the rent was low, Roger was happy there, I was just trying to think of something nice to say to Roger." Mrs. Dudak was polite and replied, "Now, Sherman, don't you apologize for a thing. It was time Roger found something better, and we're happy for him." Mr. Wolf then went outside on the deck, where he said to Mr. Wolf, "Oh, God, John, I'm so embarrassed I could crawl into a hole. I just told Roger this place was a lot better than that pig-pen he used to live in, and who was standing right there but Mrs. Dudak!" Mr. McHugh then said to Mr. Wolf, "Sherman, I don't believe you've ever met Mr. Dudak, who is sitting right here next to me. And ... Sherman? When Roger moved out of the pig-pen, I moved in."[127]

• Following a rehearsal with the London Symphony Orchestra, André Previn was having a drink in a hotel bar when he noticed an American composer he respected, so he ordered him a drink. The American composer complimented him, saying that the orchestra had sounded marvelous a few nights ago when the program included Beethoven's Sixth in the first half. Mr. Previn replied, "That was the night Pollini was supposed to play the Fourth Piano Concerto in the second half, and he canceled, and we were stuck with one of those last-minute substitutions, that really appalling third-rate lady pianist. I'm really sorry you had to suffer through that." The American composer coldly replied, "I didn't mind. The pianist is my wife."[128]

• Baritone Günter Reich once played the role of Scarpia on very short notice — so short that he had no chance for a rehearsal. When he lay dead, Tosca put a cross on his chest. Relieved that the scene was over, Mr. Reich got to his feet — only to find that the scene was not over. Knowing that the members of the audience had already seen him rise, he bowed to them, and then walked on stage. And in 1984, a production of *Das Rheingold* by Sir Peter Hall at Bayreuth featured three nude Rhein Maidens swimming in a see-through water trough. The dress dress (undress?) rehearsal was especially memorable, filled as it was with screaming nude Rhine Maidens — someone had added to the water six lively bullfrogs [129]

• In 1964, Marti Stevens played Elvira in *High Spirits*, the musical version of Noël Coward's *Blithe Spirit*. Her first scene had her speak "Good evening, Charles" through a microphone, then fly onto stage with the aid of a cable. Unfortunately, the microphone had a short circuit, and the electrical shock she received knocked her off a 12-foot platform and she swung back and forth in front of the audience before falling on her butt. After the performance, Mr. Coward went backstage and congratulated her on her performance: "I'm very proud of you. You managed to play the first act of my little comedy tonight with all the Chinese flair and light-hearted brilliance of Lady Macbeth."[130]

• A common occurrence at many classical music concerts is discovering that the program is incorrectly printed. Unfortunately, this happens even at the highest level of the music world. Famed conductor Sir Thomas Beecham once told his audience during a concert: "Ladies and gentlemen, in upwards of fifty years of concert-giving before the public, it has seldom been my good fortune to find the program correctly printed. Tonight is no exception to the rule, and therefore, with your kind permission, we will now play you the piece which you think you have just heard."[131]

• Brendan Gill of *The New Yorker* admits that when he was younger he could be a little arrogant. He says that he once trotted out a fact that he had learned from "Talk of the Town" — something such as the first person in history to read without moving his lips was Saint Ambrose. When someone asked him how he knew that, he said grandly, "I know everything." Hearing that, a beautiful Italian woman said to him, "Tell me about the Battle of Mukden." He was forced to admit that he knew nothing about the very important Battle of Mukden.[132]

• Comedian Don Knotts was once requested to emcee a dinner for fellow comedian Bob Hope. At first, Mr. Knotts was reluctant to emcee the dinner because he didn't think he was that good at emceeing, but when the very persuasive promoter of the dinner told him that Mr. Hope had specifically requested that Mr. Knotts be the emcee, he agreed. However, when he arrived at the dinner, Mr. Hope greeted him, and then asked, "Hi, Don. What are you doing here?"[133]

• Art Linkletter knew about many, many embarrassing moments. For example, the father of one family sometimes had to leave on business trips, during which the family's small children would sleep in their mother's bed. One time, however, the small children were naughty, so as punishment she made them sleep in their own beds. When the father returned home, one of the small children told him loudly at the airport, "No one slept with Mom while you were gone."[134]

• Terri Elders once enjoyed a delicious blue raspberry treat before teaching, and she was happy that her students were paying very close attention to her as she spoke. Unfortunately, after the class was over, one of her female students handed her a compact and said, "You might want to have a look." She looked, and she saw that her raspberry treat had turned her lips, tongue, and teeth blue.[135]

• Robert Morley needed to back up his brand-new Jaguar, so he asked the daughter of the Italian Prince Tasco to tell him if anything was coming. Immediately, he backed up his Jaguar into a lorry (British for a motor truck). When he reminded the Prince's daughter, "I asked you to tell me if there was anything coming," she replied, "But that wasn't coming. That was there all the time."[136]

• As a member of the Bandbox Repertory Company, Eve Arden performed in hotels, where the sets often consisted of hotel furniture in the hotel's lounge or garden. Often, Ms. Arden would appear on stage in a part, then walk to a chair — only to find it already occupied by one of the hotel's elderly guests, taking a nap.[137]

• Theatre director Michael Benthall once criticized the extras while directing a production of *Julius Caesar* at the Old Vic, saying that they weren't acting naturally. He told them, "Just behave as you would normally in a crowded street." That night, while a crowd of extras exited the stage, one of them called out, "Taxi!"[138]

Money

• A certain man wore poor clothing and always sat in the synagogue among the poorest Jews. However, when Rabbi Akiba wanted to sell a very valuable pearl, this man bought it, taking Rabbi Akiba to his house to give him the money. Rabbi Akiba was surprised to learn that the poorly dressed man had enough money to pay cash for the pearl and that he lived in such a fine house; therefore, he asked the man why he dressed in such poor clothing and always sat among the poorest Jews in the synagogue. The man replied, "Riches are not stable. Tomorrow I might lose everything. No man should, therefore, be proud. I prefer to dress poorly and to sit among the poorest Jews in the synagogue so as not to be dismayed if I should lose everything."[139]

• Xu Wenchang once visited a temple, where the chief priest, widely known for his greed, presented him with a book in order for him to record his donation to the temple. Xu Wenchang saw that other people had written such things as "Ten dollars" or "Fifteen dollars," and he wrote, "A thousand," then said his hand hurt and so he did not finish writing down his donation. The chief priest was very happy when he saw the words "A thousand" written down, and he ordered an expensive feast to be prepared. After Xu Wenchang had enjoyed the feast, the chief priest brought out the donation book again, and Xu Wenchang finished writing his donation, "A thousand pennies."[140]

• When Robert Briscoe, the Jewish mayor of Dublin, Ireland, visited Egypt, he engaged the services of a guide for a while, paying him £1 a day. Discovering that he was overpaying the guide, he fired him, then engaged a new guide for 5 shillings. Later, the guide he had fired asked to be rehired, saying that he was willing to work for 10 shillings a day. Mr. Briscoe asked, "Why should I be paying you 10 shillings when this other chap gives me good service for 5?" The guide replied, "He is a very lazy man. He has only one wife — I have three." Mr. Briscoe reengaged him. Why? "His sense of humor was worth the difference."[141]

• Being a beautiful woman has its advantages. A café-bar on Spring and Broadway in New York City gives VIP cards to the models at a particular agency; with the VIP cards, the models get 75 percent off everything. When Sara (no last name given) went to the café-bar to use the card, they told her that to get the discount she had to sit in the window so people could see her. Sara says, "They want to get more people in there who want to be around pretty girls, and they're not discreet about it at all. You definitely feel used. But, at the same time, if I can get 75 percent off, I'll go for it, you know."[142]

• In 1955, the Brooklyn Dodgers won the World Series — the only time they won. After their victory, Dodgers Carl Erskine and Duke Snider were traveling on the Pennsylvania Turnpike when a state trooper pulled them over. The trooper gave them a warning for speeding, then told them, "By the way, I lost money on you guys again this year." Mr. Erskine asked, "How did you lose money? We just won the World Series." The trooper replied, "I bet on the Dodgers in 1947, 1949, 1952, and 1953. You guys lost every one. I said nuts to them this year, and I'm betting on the Yankees."[143]

• Sylvester Stallone had guts after writing the screenplay for *Rocky*. He wanted to star in the movie, figuring that it might be his only opportunity to become a movie star, but the movie studio wanted an established star to play the character of Rocky Balboa. Although Mr. Stallone had less than $100, he turned down over $250,000 to sign away the screenplay and let someone else star in the movie. He accepted instead only $25,000 — and 10 percent of the profits, which made him millions.[144]

• In England, the Department of Inland Revenue (the equivalent of our Internal Revenue Service) shows remarkable zeal. After Thomas Beecham (died 1961) presented *A Beggar's Opera*, Inland Revenue attempted to track down its authors so it could tax them. (*A Beggar's Opera* was originally produced in 1728.) A few years afterward, Beecham produced John Fletcher's *Faithful Shepherdess*, and Inland Revenue attempted to track down Fletcher so it could tax him. (Fletcher died in 1625.)[145]

• Evil has a very difficult time tempting human beings to commit sin. Why? Before Evil can tempt anyone to commit sin, the human beings have already committed the sin! By the way, we sometimes hear that wealth is evil; however, clergyman Sydney Smith disagreed: "I read Seneca's 'On the Contempt of Wealth.' What intolerable nonsense! ... I have been very poor the greater part of my life, and have borne it as well, I believe, as most people, but I can safely say that I have been happier every guinea I have gained."[146]

• Two great American satirists — Joseph Heller, author of *Catch-22*, and Kurt Vonnegut, Jr., author of *Slaughterhouse-Five* — attended a party that a billionaire was giving. Mr. Vonnegut asked Mr. Heller, "Joe, how does it make you feel to know that our host only yesterday may have made more money than your novel *Catch-22* has earned in its entire history?" Mr. Heller replied, "I've got something he can never have: the knowledge that I've got enough."[147]

• When country comedian Jerry Clower started to become famous and make a lot of money, he was worried that it might change him, so he told his wife about the big money, "Honey, I don't know what's happening to me, but if it comes between me and you, I'll lay it down." The fame and big money turned out not to be a major problem. Mr. Clower and his wife stayed married, he tithed to his church, and he donated both money and time to charity.[148]

• To get big stars, big money is often needed. Oscar Hammerstein wanted soprano Nellie Melba to sing in his opera company, but she refused. One day Mr. Hammerstein saw her in her suite at the Grand Hotel, where once again he asked her to sing in his company. Once again, she refused. Mr. Hammerstein threw a huge handful of thousand-franc notes into the air, then left as they fluttered down over Ms. Melba. She signed a contract the following day.[149]

• Florenz "Flo" Ziegfeld frequently needed money, although he produced many money-making spectaculars in his lifetime. One day, he telegraphed comedian Ed Wynn that he needed $5,000 immediately. Mr. Wynn thought that the money must be needed for an emergency, so he wired him the money, but Mr. Ziegfeld used all of the $5,000 for a luxurious private railroad car to carry him from New York to Hollywood in style.[150]

• According to Chinese Buddhist lore, 18 solid gold lohan statues exist. One day, a farmer was farming and dug up in his field one of the 18 solid gold lohan statues. His neighbors were very happy for him, saying that he could live in ease for the rest of his life, but the farmer was sad. When his neighbors asked why he was sad, he said, "Because I don't know where the 17 other solid gold lohan statues are."[151]

• R' Meir of Lublin once spoke to raise money for his school, *Yeshivas Chachmei Lublin*. Afterwards, he saw a small child who had been in the audience and asked if he had understood the speech. The child replied, "No, I didn't. I understood only one thing: that one must give money." R' Meir smiled and said, "If you caught that, you understood my speech better than many of your elders."[152]

• A rich man asked English painter Joseph William Turner how much one of his paintings cost. When he heard the price, he said that it was an outrageous price for a piece of canvas with some paint on it. "If all you want is a piece of canvas with some paint on it," Mr. Turner said, "here is some canvas and here is some paint. Put some paint on the canvas, then take it home."[153]

• Martial arts expert and actor Bruce Lee had amazingly quick hands. He would sometimes ask a person to hold a dime in their open hand, then he would attempt to snatch the dime out of their hand before they could close it into a fist. Often, someone would think that they had beaten Mr. Lee, but when they opened their hand again, they discovered that they were holding a nickel, not a dime.[154]

• Humorist Robert Benchley signed his checks in funny ways. One of his check endorsements was even framed and hung in a bank office. The endorsement said this: "Dear Bankers Trust Company: Well, here we are in picturesque old Munich! Love to Aunt Julia, and how about Happy Hetzler, the old Hetzler? Yours in Zeta Psi, Don Stewart, and I love you, Bob Benchley."[155]

• Some boys were boasting about how much money their parents made. The son of a car salesman said that his father made $500 just for selling a used car. The son of a lawyer said that his father made $1,000 just for giving advice. The son of a preacher said, "My father gives a talk, and it takes eight people to bring him his money."[156]

• Mulla Nasrudin and the conqueror Tamburlaine were taking a Turkish bath together when Tamburlaine asked, "How much do you think I am worth?" Nasrudin answered by naming a very low sum, which shocked Tamburlaine, who said, "Why, that is the worth of the towel I am wearing!" Nasrudin replied, "I know."[157]

• Sir Thomas Beecham once bet Richard Strauss £100 that he could conduct — without a score — *Elektra*. Mr. Strauss made the bet, but he didn't pay up when Sir Thomas won. Therefore, when it was time for Mr. Strauss to be paid his royalties, Sir Thomas deducted £100 from the check.[158]

• Wally Frederick, a friend of Peg Bracken, once hosted a luncheon for 30 at the Tour d'Argent. After the luncheon, two rows of waiters appeared, with each waiter holding his hand out for a tip. Smiling broadly, Mr. Frederick walked down the two rows and shook each waiter's hand.[159]

• Rabbi Gamliel believed in giving charity cheerfully. After all, he explained, money given to the poor is not lost. God guarantees the money given to the poor, and he returns with interest in the next life what is given away in this life.[160]

Chapter 4: From Movies to Problem-Solving

Movies

• When Maury Maverick, Jr. served in the Texas House of Representatives in the 1950s, a powerful movie lobbyist named D.F. Strickland gave him a movie pass that would allow him to watch movies free in any Interstate Theater in Texas. However, Mr. Maverick felt that politicians ought not to accept such freebies, so he returned the free movie pass. Mr. Strickland wrote him this note: "Dear Mr. Maverick: I have been a lobbyist in Austin for over three decades. In all that time only one other legislator returned his movie pass, and he was a Baptist preacher who later went insane." Mr. Maverick wrote back: "Dear Mr. Strickland: Please send me back my movie pass."[161]

• Near the end of *Reservoir Dogs*, four people are shot, but if you watch the film in slow motion, you will hear only three shots. According to the script, Mr. White was supposed to fire his gun twice, but a blood squib went off too quickly, so the actor playing Mr. White fell down after firing his gun only once. The film's writer/director, Quentin Tarantino, discovered the mistake, but said, "Leave it. They'll talk about it forever." (Mr. Tarantino was right — it has been widely discussed.)[162]

• When comedian Danny Kaye was discovered by Sam Goldwyn, who saw him in the play *Lady in the Dark*, Mr. Goldwyn came backstage and said, "You're a very funny man, but if I sign you, you're going to have to have your nose fixed. It's too long." Mr. Kaye replied, "No." And his wife said, "He's doing all right with it the way it is." Mr. Goldwyn said, "It's not photogenic," so Mr. Kaye offered him a deal: "I'll have mine fixed if you have yours fixed."[163]

• In the movie-making business, the hype ground out by the PR office often far exceeds what the movie being hyped is able to deliver.

Long ago, Steve Broidy, the President of Monogram, looked at a press book — filled with superlatives — for one of his B-pictures, then said, "Why don't we put sprocket holes on the press book and throw the picture away?"[164]

• At the end of filming the movie *Jaws*, the cast and crew planned to throw director Steven Spielberg in the water, but he learned about their plot, so at the end of filming he jumped into a motor boat and sped away, shouting, "I shall *not* return!"[165]

Music

• Kristin Hersh started writing songs at age nine, but when someone asked if she was a music prodigy, she said no. Why? She explained, "They were terrible, terrible songs." When she and a couple of female friends formed the band Muses in 1982 (it was later renamed Throwing Muses), at first they did not want to have any male members of the band. But they quickly decided otherwise because they knew only one drummer, who was male. By the way, she grew up with a bunch of hippies, one of whom wanted to paint the phrase "Be together" on the roof of the commune's barn. However, he wrote "Be a tog eater" instead. Kristin's father signed his letters to her, "Be a tog eater. Love, Dad."[166]

• When Walter Damrosch's *Cyrano de Bergerac* was presented by the Metropolitan Opera, many opera-knowledgeable people discerned passages that seemed more than reminiscent of passages written by other composers. At a rehearsal, Frances Alda finished singing an aria, then asked, "Where do we go from here?" The assistant conductor replied, "From Gounod to Meyerbeer." At another rehearsal, Ms. Alda saw another singer listening to the score of *Cyrano de Bergerac* and frequently bowing to the air. Curious, she asked him, "What are you doing?" He replied, "I am saluting the spirits of the dead masters." (The opera was not a success.)[167]

• Corey Ford was a stringer for *The New York Times* while he was attending Columbia University; he really did keep himself very busy, even composing and sending in a football song to a contest at Columbia. One day, a *Times* editor called him up, wondering why he had not written an article on the winner of the football song contest. The editor ordered Mr. Ford to interview the winner. Looking at his notes, the editor said, "Damn it, it's you." And that's how Mr. Ford found out that he had won the contest.[168]

• Joan Jett's parents supported her; for one thing, for Christmas they gave her a guitar — her first. When she was a teenager, she told her mother that she wanted to join a rock band: "Ma, this is something I really want to do, and I'm going to do it, no matter what — but I would really rather do it with your blessing." Her parents supported her, and they told her, "Go ahead. Just be safe and let us know what you're doing and where you are." Ms. Jett says, "They were always just so cool about it."[169]

• In 1835, Theobald Boehm designed a new flute that allowed musicians to play compositions that had previously been impossible for one musician to play. He took his new invention to composer Gioacchino Rossini and demonstrated it. Rossini was amazed and said, "You cannot play that!" Mr. Boehm pointed out that in fact he was playing it, but Rossini insisted, "I don't care if you are — it is utterly impossible."[170]

• Jazz pianist Marion McPartland sometimes took requests, but sometimes fans made requests that were not in her current repertoire. While she was playing at New York's Tavern on the Green, a fan requested "Melancholy Baby." Because it was not in her current repertoire, she said, "We do that in the third set" — but at the Tavern on the Green she was playing only two sets.[171]

• Many opera singers grow fat. One of Gioacchino Rossini's star singers, contralto Marietta Alboni, grew too fat to sing opera because she couldn't move and sing at the same time. She had to make her living giving concerts at which she sang while seated in an armchair.

Mr. Rossini referred to her as "the elephant who swallowed a nightingale."[172]

• A preacher talked about praising God through song and mentioned a few of his favorite hymns, then he asked the children of the congregation for their favorite hymns. One young boy said, "From the land of sky-blue waters" — which was the beginning of a jingle from a TV commercial for beer.[173]

Names

• Gummo Marx was in show business with the famous Marx Brothers before they started making movies, but he left show business to go into manufacturing women's clothing. When Bobby, his son, returned from his first day of kindergarten, Gummo asked what the kids had done. Bobby said that all the kids had talked about their fathers and what they did for a living. Gummo asked, "Did you say that I was in show business?" Bobby answered, "Yes, but I said that your name is Harpo." Gummo said, "Bobby, you know my name." Bobby replied, "Of course, Daddy, but whoever heard of Gummo Marx?"[174]

• When Mary McLeod Bethune was a small schoolchild, she was impressed that her teacher insisted on being called "Miss Wilson." In the Jim Crow south, honorary titles such as "Mr.," "Mrs.," and "Miss" were used mainly by white people. As an adult, Ms. Bethune wanted white people whom she did not know well to call her "Mrs. Bethune."[175]

Parents

• Robert Benchley's mother once needed a passport. She went to the appropriate office, and the official told her to raise her right hand, then he asked, "Do you swear to defend the Constitution of the United States against all enemies, domestic and foreign?" Mrs. Benchley, whose eldest son had died fighting in the Spanish-American War, was startled. She lowered her hand, then asked, "Do I have to?" The official replied, "If you want a passport, you do." Mrs. Benchley said, "Well, there are days when I wouldn't." Then she took the oath.[176]

• Maria Shriver spoke at the funeral of her mother, Eunice Shriver, who managed to get a lot done during her long life. Maria remembered once when her mother picked her up after school: Eunice was wearing a sweater on which were pinned several scraps of paper. Together, the scraps of paper formed a to-do list. On each scrap of paper Eunice had written a task that she wanted to do by the end of the day.[177]

• Robert Klein's father used to joke during the Seder at the beginning of Passover. When he was asked, "Why is this night different from all other nights?" he would answer, "Because yesterday was Thursday and today is Friday."[178]

Police

• The Pope's airplane arrived late in Chicago, where His Holiness was going to speak, so the Pope jumped into a taxi and told the driver that there would be a $100 tip for him if he got the Pope at his destination on time. However, hearing the destination, the taxi driver was dubious that he could make it there on time, so the Pope offered him the $100 if he would let the Pope drive. This was agreeable, so the Pope took over the steering wheel and the taxi driver rode in the back seat. Unfortunately, the Pope's speeding was noticed by a police officer, who stopped the taxi and was astonished to see His Holiness driving. The police officer called his superiors and reported that he had stopped a very big VIP. He was asked, "Is he a city council person?" The police officer replied, "Bigger." He was asked, "Is he the Mayor?" The police officer replied, "Bigger." He was asked, "Is he the Governor?" The police officer replied, "Bigger." Finally, he was asked, "Who is he?" The police officer replied, "I don't know, but the Pope is his chauffeur."[179]

• Actress Eve Arden once got in her car and was preparing to go to work. However, a police car stopped beside her and an officer asked, "Going somewhere, lady?" Ms. Arden replied, "Yes, I'm going to work."

The officer said, "Not in that car, lady. Get out and look at it." She did, and discovered that three of the car's wheels had been taken off and the car was sitting on blocks.[180]

• During the 1913-1914 strike by union coal miners in Colorado, union organizer Mother Jones was arrested. The soldier arresting the old woman asked her, "Will you take my arm, madam?" Mother Jones snapped back, "No, I won't — you take my suitcase."[181]

Practical Jokes

• Roger Ebert had a great admiration for actress Katherine Harrold. When he and Gene Siskel were reviewing on TV a horror movie she had starred in, Mr. Ebert thought that she was very effective and Mr. Siskel accused him of being partial to her and said to him, "Instead of reviewing her movie, why don't you ask her to dinner?" Soon afterward, a letter arrived from Ms. Harrold, saying to Mr. Ebert that she had enjoyed the review and inviting him to go out to dinner with her the next time he was in New York. Mr. Ebert asked Mr. Siskel if he had written the letter as a practical joke. Mr. Siskel said that yes, he had. But the real practical joke was that Mr. Siskel had NOT written the letter.[182]

• In Stamford (Connecticut) High School, actor Bob Crane was a joker. He would go into his girlfriend's typing class and pretend he was a member of the class, although it was a female-only class. In addition, before playing Colonel Robert Hogan on TV's *Hogan's Heroes*, Mr. Crane had been an irreverent radio show host who frequently made fun of his sponsors. While playing a commercial for cigarettes, for example, he would also play a recording of a man coughing, and while playing a commercial for an airline, he would also play a recording of an airplane with a sputtering engine.[183]

• Fans of old movies remember Basil Rathbone's portrayal of Sherlock Holmes and Nigel Bruce's portrayal of Dr. Watson. The two actors also played those roles on a radio series. When they arrived at the radio studio each day, they carried in a snack of Danish and milk. When the snack was over, Mr. Rathbone and Mr. Bruce amused themselves by throwing the leftover Danish at the radio director, Glenhall Taylor. Although Mr. Taylor was safely behind the glass window of the control room, his reflexes made him duck each week.[184]

• Author Scott Beach knew a musician who once stretched a surgical glove over the top of her bassoon and then stuffed the glove inside it. During the rehearsal, nothing seemed out of the ordinary until she played a low B-flat, which inflated the glove, making it appear as though a hand were coming out of her bassoon.[185]

Prayer

• Syndicated columnist Connie Schultz once asked a pastor, "Do we really need a set of rules or an intermediary for God to hear us?" The pastor told her a Jewish story about a farmer who was unable to arrive on time at the temple for a prayer that was traditionally prayed by a group of people only. The farmer bowed his head, and in a prayer, he recited the letters of the alphabet. Then he continued his prayer, "God, I trust you to put the letters in the right place."[186]

• A man once went into his small daughter's bedroom and asked, "Are you going to say your prayers?" She said, "I'm saying them." The father then said, "I can't hear you," and his daughter replied, "I'm not talking to you."[187]

Prejudice

• Veruca Salt's Louise Post remembers prejudice at a country club in the suburbs of St. Louis when she was growing up. One of her cousins brought a three-year-old black kid as a guest, and the country club officials made the black kid leave. Ms. Post's family resigned from the country club. People and institutions can change for the better. Ten years later, Ms. Post was in a Rhythm and Blues band that played at the same country club — she was the band's only white member. She says, "It felt really good to return there with that band and be paid to play."[188]

• Lionel Hampton, a black man, often performed with Benny Goodman, a white man. Mr. Goodman often invited Mr. Hampton to ride in his car with him — at a time when taxis often did not pick up black passengers. Mr. Goodman also once threatened to "bust the head" of a racist who was directing hate speech at Mr. Hampton.[189]

Problem-Solving

• When Saul was the King of Israel, a beautiful woman's wealthy husband died, and the greedy governor of the province in which she lived wished to marry her. The beautiful woman did not wish to marry the greedy governor, and she decided to flee the province until the greedy governor died. To do so, she would have to leave her gold coins behind, hidden where she hoped no one would find them. Therefore, she put the gold coins in honey jars. She filled the honey jars with gold coins partway, then filled them the rest of the way with honey to hide the gold coins. She left the jars in a storeroom of a neighbor, then fled from the region and the governor. Unfortunately, while she was away, the neighbor ran out of honey and decided to use some of her honey, thus discovering the gold coins. Becoming as greedy as the governor, he removed all of the gold coins and replaced them with honey. After the governor died, the beautiful woman returned to the province and asked for her jars of "honey" back. Of course, she was upset when the jars of "honey" were found to be filled with — of all things! — honey. Unfortunately, the greedy neighbor told her that she had left honey with him and he had returned honey to her. Seeking justice, the woman went to King Saul, who quickly discovered that she had no witnesses that gold coins had been in the jars, so he dismissed her. She left the court, weeping, and a shepherd boy asked why she was crying. When she explained the matter to him, the shepherd boy said that he could help her, and he returned with her to King Saul, who gave him permission to investigate the case. The shepherd boy went to the honey jars and smashed them, then he looked at the broken shards. Picking up one of the shards, he showed it to King Saul. Glued to the shard — with honey — were two gold coins. After seeing this evidence that the woman's story was true, King Saul ordered the greedy neighbor to return the woman's gold coins. Who was the shepherd boy? You probably have already guessed that he was David, a future King of Israel.[190]

• Arturo Toscanini felt strongly about music and how it should be played. Once he rehearsed a French orchestra whose playing was out of time. To make a point, Toscanini reached in his pocket, took out his watch, then hurled it against a wall. Frances Alda, an opera singer who was present at the rehearsal, retrieved the much-damaged watch and gave it back to Toscanini, who pocketed it. Rehearsal started again, and for a while the orchestra played well, then it began to play out of time again. Toscanini again hurled his watch against a wall, Ms. Alda again retrieved it, and Toscanini again pocketed it. After this second demonstration, the orchestra concentrated and played both in time and in tune.[191]

• In Washington, D.C., Sojourner Truth often took streetcars to get where she needed to go. However, because she was an African American, often the streetcars would not stop for her unless white people also were waiting for a ride. Once, several streetcars passed by her although she signaled for them to stop. Finally, Ms. Truth started shouting, louder and louder, "I want to ride! *I want to ride! I WANT TO RIDE!*" The elderly black woman attracted so much attention to herself that pedestrians stopped and traffic stopped—including a streetcar. Ms. Truth then quieted down and boarded the streetcar. Several passengers were amused at how she had tricked the streetcar driver into stopping.[192]

• Pioneers traveling west in covered wagons across North America faced a race against time. They started traveling from the east in the spring, and they needed to be in their new homesteads out west before winter set in. The travel was difficult, and the pioneers had to become accustomed to new things. For example, on the treeless prairies, wood was rare. Therefore, pioneers had to learn to cook over fires made by burning dried buffalo dung. Without trees, privacy was hard to come by when answering calls of nature. Therefore, pioneer women used to stand together and spread their skirts out to give privacy to a woman performing a bathroom function.[193]

• Author Robert Canzoneri had a major problem to solve. His dog, Bear, coveted Piggy, a toy that belonged to Niki, Robert's two-year-old granddaughter. When Niki was finished playing with her toys and ready for a nap, she would put her toys in a pile. When Niki was asleep, Bear would go to the pile, find Piggy, and hide it. Niki would wake up, and then she would look through the house until she had found Piggy. Fortunately, Niki's parents found another squeaky pig that was identical to Piggy, so Niki and Bear no longer had to share the toy.[194]

• Juliette Gordon Low, founder of the Girls Scouts in 1912, had a deaf ear that she put to very good use. She once approached Rose Kerr about founding a group of Girl Guides (the name of the Girl Scouts during their first year of existence) in England. Ms. Kerr protested, "I cannot possibly do it. I have no time. I do not live in London. I am no good with girls." Ms. Low, with her deaf ear turned toward Ms. Kerr, replied, "Then it is settled. The next meeting is on Thursday, and I have told them that you will take it." Ms. Kerr took the meeting and started the new troop of Girl Guides.[195]

• Ohio State University football coach Woody Hayes valued punctuality. One day, it seemed as if he was going to be late for a meeting. He drove (a little fast) into the parking lot, which seemed to be filled, and finally he found a spot where his car could fit. He maneuvered his car into the spot, but then he found that he couldn't open his door enough to get out of his car. Woody then moved his car forward, put it in neutral, got out of his car, and then pushed it back into the parking spot. He made it to the meeting on time.[196]

• Daniel Webster once got into trouble as a boy when he went to school with dirty hands. The schoolmaster said that Daniel would be whipped on the palm of a hand as his punishment, so he asked Daniel to hold out his hand. Daniel spat on his hand, wiped it on his pants, then held it out. The schoolmaster looked at the hand, then said, "Daniel, if you show me a dirtier hand than that in the school, I won't whip you." Daniel showed the schoolmaster his other hand.[197]

• At the beginning of World War II, General George S. Patton worked in the tank corps. The army was very slow in sending needed replacement parts for the tanks, so when General Patton learned from a mechanic that the parts could be easily adapted from items in the Sears Roebuck catalog, he ordered the items, paying for them out of his own money.[198]

• Opera singer Risë Stevens was being driven to a performance when she noticed that the chauffeur was drunk and driving unsafely. Thinking quickly, she asked the chauffeur to stop to get her a hamburger, and after the chauffeur got out of the car, she jumped behind the steering wheel and drove off, leaving the chauffeur behind.[199]

• Author Peg Bracken knew a woman who grew tired of trying to force her children to eat such breakfast foods as fruit juice, hot oatmeal, and scrambled or fried eggs. She solved her problem by allowing her children to eat applesauce, oatmeal-raisin cookies, and hard-boiled eggs for breakfast. Her children loved it.[200]

• Werner Klemperer used to wear a monocle while playing Colonel Wilhelm Klink on TV's *Hogan's Heroes*, but it took him a while to learn how to wear it, so in the early episodes the monocle was glued to his eye.[201]

Chapter 5: From Profanity to Work

Profanity

• William R. Braddock, Esq., of Medford, New Jersey, was a Quaker and he disliked swearing. While he was writing a deed for two men, they began to argue, and as they argued, they swore at each other. Mr. Braddock told the men that he did not permit swearing in his establishment, and for a while the two men stopped swearing. But again they began to argue, and again they began to swear. Mr. Braddock stopped writing the deed, told his daughter to open the door, then he grabbed each man by the back of the neck and hurled them both into the street. The two men had not had time to get their hats, so they hired a neighborhood boy to go back and pick up their hats for them.[202]

• A comedian was telling an off-color joke at an officers' club when he suddenly noticed that sitting at the table was a chaplain. "For Christ's sake," he said. "Are you a chaplain?" The chaplain replied, "For the sake of Christ, I am."[203]

Public Speaking

• Susan B. Anthony was once mocked by abolitionist Samuel May because she spoke about marriage although she was unmarried. Ms. Anthony responded by asking, "Mr. May, if you are not a slave why are you campaigning against slavery?"[204]

• Sir Winston Churchill knew that he was a great orator. When he wrote his speeches, he wrote notes where he anticipated the crowd's responses; for example, he would write such notes as "Cheers," "Ovation," and "Prolonged cheering."[205]

Publicity Stunts

• Theatrical impresario Florenz "Flo" Ziegfeld knew how to get publicity. One of his first stars was French singer Anna Held. Word leaked out to the newspapers that Mr. Ziegfeld was being sued because he had failed to pay his milk bill. Word also leaked out that Mr.

Ziegfeld was buying so much milk that it took six cows to provide his daily order. Enterprising reporters investigated, and they heard that Ms. Held was taking baths in the milk! This provided much publicity that helped make French star Anna Held a star in the United States. Of course, this was just a publicity stunt. Ms. Held did not take baths in milk — doing that would have made her sticky! Mr. Ziegfeld did not buy that much milk, and he paid a milk dealer to sue him. Playwright Max Marcin had read about ancient Roman milk baths, and Mr. Ziegfeld paid him $250 for the idea of the publicity stunt.[206]

• As a publicity stunt, Art Linkletter was supposed to broadcast on the CBS Radio Network the arrival of the United States Navy's Pacific Fleet at the 1935 San Diego Exhibition. Unfortunately, as the time drew near for the arrival of the fleet, heavy fog began to roll into the San Diego harbor, forcing the fleet to remain at anchor outside the harbor. Mr. Linkletter was faced with a problem. He had lots of time to fill on the radio, and he hated to lose such a good publicity stunt. So Mr. Linkletter simply pretended that the fleet was sailing into the harbor and described to his radio audience the destroyers and battleships that were actually nowhere to be seen.[207]

Quakers

• Stan Banker is a Quaker who attends the Middleroad Friends Meeting in Springport, Indiana. On the cover of his book about becoming a Quaker, *Walk Cheerfully the Middleroad*, is written, "Two roads diverged in a woods, and I — I took the one in the middle. And that has made all the difference." By the way, according to Mr. Banker, effective preaching has three rules: "1) Preach about God; 2) Preach about 20 minutes; and 3) If you forget one of the first two parts, make sure it is not the second part."[208]

• Back when the Erie Canal was being dug in the state of New York, several Quakers invested in the construction of the canal. Afterward, the canal was fiercely opposed at a meeting by a man who argued that if God had wanted a waterway put there, He would have done so, and it was not for Humankind to do what God had not wanted to do. The Quakers were silent for a time after the fierce attack, then one of the Quakers quoted from the Bible, "And Jacob digged a well."[209]

Rabbis

• Two rabbis argued about a matter of law. Rabbi Eliezer argued well, and all the rabbis listening to the two rabbis arguing were convinced that he was right, but Rabbi Judah still disagreed. Rabbi Eliezer said, "I am right, and that carob tree will prove it." Immediately, the carob tree uprooted itself, flew through the air 100 cubits, and rooted itself again. Rabbi Eliezer then said, "I am right, and that stream will prove it." The flowing stream immediately stopped, reversed course, and began flowing uphill. Next, Rabbi Eliezer said, "I am right, and the walls of this synagogue will prove it." The walls of the synagogue then began to lean inward dangerously, but stopped before collapsing although the laws of physics decreed that they should collapse. Finally, Rabbi Eliezer said, "I am right, and a voice from above will prove it." A voice came from Heaven and said, "In all matters, the law agrees with Rabbi Eliezer." However, Rabbi Judah was not convinced by the miracles, and he pleaded, "Listen to me, God and my fellow sages. The Torah itself tells us that it is no longer in Heaven, but was given to the people at Mount Sinai. It is our guide. In our study and discussion of its laws, we reach our decisions. That is how we govern ourselves." Rabbi Reuven agreed: "That's true. The Torah itself says we have to agree on our decisions by a majority. The law is in the hands of the court and not in the hands of one single person, even though that person may be the learned sage Rabbi Eliezer." Years later, Rabbi Reuven saw the prophet Elijah in a marketplace, and he asked what God thought of the argument between the two rabbis, the miracles, and how matters of the law ought to be decided. Elijah said, "God was pleased to see that the scholars were not so frightened by the miracles that they would give up their responsibility to discuss and decide the laws together as a court. It is true that Rabbi Eliezer was right in the argument — but it is also true that decisions about the law are made on earth, so that people may learn and grow by them."[210]

• Sometimes, children can be cruel. At one Catholic school, some parents could afford to buy their children's textbooks, but other parents could not afford to buy their children's textbooks. The school therefore allowed some children to borrow the necessary textbooks, but the textbooks that had to be returned at the end of the school year had a red sticker on them. Soon, children knew what the red stickers meant and taunted the children whose books had red stickers. A nun named Sister Rosamunde noticed this and solved the problem by requiring all the children to give her their textbooks, and then she placed a red sticker on every textbook.[211]

• A hassid asked a rebbe what is the most difficult thing in the world, and what is the easiest thing in the world. The rebbe replied, "The easiest thing in the world is to recognize your neighbors' faults. The most difficult thing in the world is to recognize your own faults."[212]

Revenge

• Hollywood screenwriter Charles MacArthur was angry at his movie studio, and he got revenge. While buying gas at a service station one day, he noticed that the attendant had a thick English accent. After discovering that the man was making $30 a week, he told him that he knew a better way to make a living. He then took him to the movie studio, introduced him as a well-known English novelist and friend of George Bernard Shaw, and very quickly the service-station attendant was hired as a $1,000-a-week screenwriter. Mr. MacArthur coached him on what to say at meetings (very little), and the gas station attendant managed to stay hired for a year without anyone finding out that he didn't know how to write.[213]

• A man called a biological supply store and asked for immediate delivery of 10,000 cockroaches. The store was able to fill the order, but the salesperson asked the man why he needed so many cockroaches.

The man replied, "I am moving out of my apartment, and my lease says that I have to leave it exactly as it was when I moved in."[214]

Telegrams

• After Igor Stravinsky scored a great success with his *Scènes de Ballet* in the Broadway production *Seven Lively Arts*, impresario Billy Rose sent him this telegram: "Your music great success. Could be sensational success if you would authorize Robert Russell Bennett to retouch the orchestration. Bennett orchestrates even the works of Cole Porter." Mr. Stravinsky sent this telegram in reply: "Satisfied with great success."[215]

• Actor Patrick Macnee once received this telegram inviting him to star in a production of *A Midsummer's Night Dream*: "Doing a production of 'The Dream.' Hear you've become a fat lush. Lose weight and you're in."[216]

Television

• The British tongue-in-cheek TV series *The Avengers* had a number of rules created by writer/producer Brian Clemens. The only class shown on *The Avengers* was the upper class. To prevent the show from clashing with reality, no uniformed policemen or ordinary people waiting for a bus were ever shown. Sex was never blatant on the series. Blood was almost never shown. A directive of the series was never to kill a woman character — but this was occasionally violated. According to Mr. Clemens, "We don't regard ourselves as a violent show. Perhaps that is why psychiatrists have said we have the ideal presentation of violence for children. We try to achieve the effect that once an actor has been killed, he gets up, collects his money and goes home."[217]

• Alan Hale, who played the Skipper on the TV series *Gilligan's Island*, was a big, strong man. In one episode, he was supposed to carry a treasure chest filled with cannonballs. Huffing and puffing, two propmen carried in the chest. During the filming of the episode, Mr. Hale picked up the chest with one hand, carried it to where it was supposed to go, then tossed it about four feet. After the director yelled

"Cut," the two propmen asked Bob Denver, who played Gilligan, if he had taken out the cannonballs. Mr. Denver shook his head no. When the propmen opened the chest, they found — cannonballs. Huffing and puffing, the two propmen carried the chest off the set.[218]

• Actor Patrick Macnee had a chance to display his riding ability in the *Avengers* episode "Silent Dust." He actually rode the same horse that Sir Laurence Olivier had ridden in *Henry V* when he made the speech "Once more into the breach, dear friends." Then, the horse was two years old. At the time of the filming of the *Avengers* episode, the horse was 22, but still wonderful. Diana Rigg also rode on a horse, but during filming she confessed to Mr. Macnee that she had never been on a horse until the day before yesterday. When he asked what she had done the day before yesterday, she replied, "I went and had a lesson."[219]

• Howard McNear played Floyd the barber on *The Andy Griffith Show*. He suffered a stroke in 1963, then retired from the show for the next two years. In 1965, he returned to the series, which made accommodations for the effects of the stroke, which had paralyzed Mr. McNear's left side. Floyd the barber was never shown walking, and he was usually shown sitting down. A special supporting structure was built so that he could be shown standing behind the barber chair.[220]

Thanksgiving

• Karleena Carpenter has cerebral palsy, and she has a service dog named Amanda to help her be independent. The dog will bring things to her, pick up things she has dropped, press a button to answer the telephone, and even open a door by tugging on a towel tied to the door handle. One Thanksgiving Karleena visited her brother and sister-in-law, and Amanda went outside to a patio. Unfortunately, the patio is where her brother and sister-in-law had placed a container of turkey so it could cool. Soon, there was no turkey but there was a very happy and very full Amanda. Karleena says, "My brother and sister-in-law were not very happy, but I thought it was pretty smart of

Amanda to open the tight lid on that container. She's very intelligent, funny, and loving."[221]

Theater

• Early in his career, Peter Ustinov appeared in a play with a star who had been chosen to act as himself on stage. When the star asked Mr. Ustinov what he was going to do in the next scene, Mr. Ustinov replied that he was going to do nothing. The star objected, "No! I'm the star. In this scene *I* do nothing."[222]

• Gladys Cooper complained that Noël Coward believed that actors should show up at the first rehearsal knowing their lines, whereas she liked to learn her lines during rehearsals. Mr. Coward told her, "I did not expect word perfection at the first rehearsal, but I had rather hoped for it on the first night."[223]

Travel

• Young people's author Richard Peck was born in Decatur, Illinois, but he knew that he wanted to go to New York. When he was in kindergarten, his teacher would play a song on the piano while the children marched around the room. One day, young Richard requested "Sidewalks of New York." When her teacher asked why he had requested that song, he replied, "Because I'll be moving there." Because she knew that his parents liked living in Decatur, she asked, "Soon?" He replied, "Well, as soon as I can get there." When Richard was 16, a relative invited him to go to New York. Richard liked New York, and he was happy to learn that "the outside world was really there and somewhat better than the movies." In addition, he says, "It occurred to me that this was the place that I'd been homesick for all along."[224]

• Cellist Yo-Yo Ma owns some very expensive musical instruments, and of course when he travels, he can't simply put a Stradivarius in the cargo hold of an airplane. Therefore, he pays an extra fare to carry his instruments on board. Once, a person at the ticket booth could not find the reservation Mr. Ma had made for his instrument. Mr. Ma asked to look at the reservation list, and he discovered that the reservation was made under "Mr. Cabinba" — which is short for cabin baggage. (Because of Mr. Ma's heavy travel schedule, he has practiced in airports, on board ship, and even once on the Autobahn after his car broke down.)[225]

• Choreographer Lynne Taylor Corbett was in Israel a week after the Six Days' War, and she remembers seeing a neighborhood in Jerusalem where Jews and Arabs met and talked together. Although the war had just been fought, in this neighborhood the two sides were at peace. She thought, "Isn't this great? They have finally found peace!" Although the conflict between the two groups has continued, she says that "the memory of these sworn enemies interacting peacefully stayed with me."[226]

• Maxim Gorky once stayed at a hotel in Southern Italy. The next morning, he complained that he had not been able to sleep at night because his bed was infested. His landlady denied the charge, saying, "We have not a single bug in this house." Mr. Gorky replied, "That is true. The bugs are not single — they are married and have very large families, too."[227]

• Pioneers on the almost treeless plains rejoiced when they saw a rare tree. A pioneer couple once traveled a long distance to collect wood, and when the woman saw a tree, she wrapped her arms around it and cried — the last time she had seen a tree was two years previously.[228]

• While traveling in Ireland, Peg Bracken rode in a car behind a bus bearing this difficult-to-read sign: "To Read This Sign, Hold Bus Upside Down."[229]

Wisdom

• R' Yonasan of Prague was a friend to the king, and the king asked him before setting out to war if R' Yonasan could tell which of the two gates of the city he would use when he returned from war. R' Yonasan said that he would not answer the question right now, because whatever gate he mentioned, the king could easily decide to go through the other gate. Instead, he would write down his answer, then seal it so that the answer could not be read, and after the king had returned to the city, he could break the seal and read the answer. The king agreed and carried the answer with him to the war. Returning from the war, the king decided to trick R' Yonasan and not use either gate to enter the city; instead, he ordered that the wall be breached and a third gate be built, and he entered the city through that. After entering the city by way of the new gate, the king broke the seal and read a quotation from the Gemara: "A king may breach a wall to make a path for himself" (Bava Basra 100b).[230]

• A man visited Zhu Gongmin, a famous and wise scholar. The man decided to test Zhu Gongmin, so he said, "You are famous for being wise. Can you make me leave the house?" Zhu Gongmin replied, "I don't want to do that because it is so cold outside; however, if you were outside, I could make you come inside." The man went outside. Zhu Gongmin then laughed at the man and said, "I made you go outside."[231]

• The Jews of Galicia often spent much money decorating their sukkos, a custom that Rabbi Chaim of Sanz opposed because he felt that it was a wasteful practice. Rabbi Chaim spent little money decorating his sukkah; instead, he donated more money to feed the poor, saying, "The best sukkah decoration is to ensure that the poor do not go hungry during the festival."[232]

Wit

• Sir Thomas Beecham, the noted conductor, was a wit who said many things that are still remembered today. He once told a critic, "You know, my dear fellow, you belong to a fraternity that has almost a genius for stating what is exactly opposite to the true facts." Once, some university members were discussing setting up a new chair of musical criticism. Sir Thoma, said, "If there is to be a chair for critics, I think it should be an electric chair." The Royal Albert Hall is famous for its echo, leading Sir Thomas to say, "British composers should all endeavor to have their works performed in this hall; they will thus be assured of at least two performances." Sir Thomas also was very blunt and once when a noisy audience at a Covent Garden concert performance of *Fidelio* annoyed him, he suddenly whirled around, faced the audience, and shouted, "Stop talking!"[233]

• During World War I, Charles MacArthur served as a private in the United States Army, where he got bored with saluting officers and calling them "sir." So Mr. MacArthur and his friends each day elected a private to serve as caliph for the day. Before addressing the caliph, each person had to bow to him twice and then use only high-falutin' language such as "O Commander of the Faithful, is it true that ...."[234]

Work

• Cindy Margolis took action to get what she wanted. She could not get a modeling agent, so she told herself, "I'm gonna do this myself." She created her own greeting cards, using herself as the model for the photographs. She admits that the greeting cards were "really, really, cheesy," and the photographs were really, really cheesecake. For example, one photograph showed her in a police uniform along with the slogan "Go ahead. Make my day." She was successful, and America Online put her photograph online. AOL even told her, "You broke all these download records. Seventy thousand in twenty-four hours. Every ten seconds, someone was downloading you." She has her own Web site, and mothers e-mail her to say, "Thank you for having a clean site. I don't mind if my son comes to your site." Ms. Margolis points out, "My site is completely PG rated. I've never posed nude. If they want a sweet, sexy girl next door, then they come to my site. Everything is 100 percent me."[235]

• While serving in the United States Army in Germany, Richard Peck noticed that the soldiers were bored by the chaplain's sermon, so he wrote a sermon that he knew would address a topic that the soldiers were interested in, and he slipped it under the chaplain's door. He was happy when the chaplain delivered it the next Sunday, so he wrote another sermon. This time, he made sure that he was caught when he slipped the sermon under the chaplain's door, and he became the chaplain's assistant. Not only did he write the chaplain's sermons, but he also counseled the soldiers, an experience that helped him when he became an author of novels for young people.[236]

• At times people need to work together to accomplish something major. To create the Stravinsky Festival of 1972, members of the New York City Ballet worked together. New ballets were created, and the members worked long hours to learn and rehearse those ballets. No one complained about the constant breaking of union rules. Everyone was overworked, and no one shirked their work because if they had, the work would have had to be done by another already overworked person. This was the result: an incredibly successful festival and several new ballet masterpieces.[237]

• Robert Benchley's first secretary was Charles MacGregor, one of whose jobs was to get Mr. Benchley out of bed. This he did in various ways, such as walking into Mr. Benchley's bedroom and saying, "The men are here for the trunks." This news awoke Mr. Benchley immediately, and by the time he realized that no men had come for the trunks, it was impossible for him to go back to sleep. On another occasion, Mr. MacGregor woke Mr. Benchley by saying, "There are some men here to flood the bed for skating."[238]

• Choreographer Moses Pendleton enjoys coffee that is sweetened with maple syrup. He also has unusual qualifications that he looks for in the dancers he uses in his work. He looks for, first, "a quality in that person that catches your eye and makes you want to follow them." The second quality is also very important. He says, "The other important requirement is that they appreciate the humor of their director. If they laugh at my jokes, then they're in."[239]

• Allan Ramsay was a portraitist who used assistants to paint the less important parts of his paintings. Normally, he painted the faces and hands himself, leaving the rest of his work to his assistants.

However, after his pupil Philip Reinagle showed himself worthy, Mr. Ramsay began to let him paint the faces and hands. This means that Mr. Ramsay did not do any of the actual painting of many works of art that bear his name in museums.[240]

• Comedian Howard Storm once worked at a nightclub in Youngstown, Ohio, when a man walked in and started shooting. Of course, Mr. Storm got out of the room as quickly as possible and ran to the nightclub's owner, Shakey Naples, to explain what was happening. Mr. Naples asked, "Is he shootin' at you?" Mr. Storm replied, "No," and Mr. Naples told him, "Well, then get back onstage and do your act."[241]

• Action movie star Jean-Claude Van Damme worked for a while as a limo driver. Once, a customer — the publisher of a big magazine — asked him if he could drive from the airport to Malibu in 20 minutes. Mr. Van Damme did it, flooring the gas pedal and driving through red lights. When he got to Malibu, he opened the door for the magazine publisher, who told him, "You drive too fast" — and did not give him a tip.[242]

• Johann Sebastian Bach spent some time in jail. Why? When Mr. Bach was an organist at Weimar, the arguing that went on between the Duke and the Duke's nephew bothered him, so he accepted a job offer from Prince Leopold of Anhalt-Cöthen. Because of "too obstinately requesting his dismissal," Bach was put in jail for a month, during which time he composed 46 chorale preludes.[243]

• Film director Gabriel Pascal once called Robert Morley's agent and urged that Mr. Morley take a cut in pay for the film they were making together. Mr. Morley's agent declined to reduce his client's salary, saying, "If Morley is as bad as you say, he would be very unwise to take a cut in salary as obviously he will never work again."[244]

• At the Haymarket Theatre, an old man called Bibby worked as the stage door keeper, but a better employee for the position should have been found. One night, the play was running late, so Bibby, who was tired of waiting, walked on stage, gave the keys to the lead actor, and told him to lock up when the play was over.[245]

• Freddie Fox, a stutterer, wrote comedy for Bob Hope. Mr. Hope formed the habit of calling Mr. Fox at all hours for jokes, and Mr. Fox got tired of this habit. On the telephone, Mr. Fox said, "Bbbbob, you ttttake your jjjjob and ssssh ...." Mr. Hope said, "It's OK, Fred; I get the idea," then hung up.[246]

• Not all singers in church congregations are talented. A New York churchgoer sang the closing hymn with the rest of the congregation, but afterward a visitor turned to the singer and joked, "Don't give up your day job."[247]

• What does it take to be a top stand-up comedian? The Library of Congress once hosted an exhibit titled "Bob Hope and American Variety." Among the items on display were 85,000 pages of jokes![248]

• Noël Coward once told reporter Robert Robinson, "One day I will retire from public life." When asked when that day would be, Mr. Coward replied, "You may follow my coffin."[249]

• Backstage, comedian Buddy Flanagan watched an acrobatic act energetically perform, and then he said, "Look at those silly so-and-so's — too lazy to learn a comic song."[250]

Appendix A: Bibliography

Adams, Joey. *The God Bit*. Boston, MA: G.K. Hall & Co., 1975.

Adir, Karen. *The Great Clowns of American Television*. Jefferson, NC: McFarland & Company, Inc., 1988.

Adler, Bill. *Jewish Wit and Wisdom*. New York: Dell Publishing Co., Inc, 1969.

Aflaki, Shams al-Din Ahmad. *Legends of the Sufis: Selected Anecdotes from the Work Entitled, The Acts of the Adepts by Shemsu-'D-Din Ahmed, El Eflaki*. London: Theosophical Publishing House, 1976.

Alda, Frances. *Men, Women, and Tenors*. Boston, MA: Houghton Mifflin Company, 1937.

Alley, Ken. *Awkward Christian Soldiers*. Wheaton, IL: Harold Shaw Publishers, 1998.

Arden, Eve. *Three Phases of Eve: An Autobiography*. New York: St. Martin's Press, 1985.

Ashley, Merrill. *Dancing for Balanchine*. New York: E.P. Dutton, Inc., 1984.

Atkins, Harold and Archie Newman, compilers. *Beecham Stories*. Great Britain: Futura Publications, Limited, 1978.

Aurand, Jr., A. Monroe. *Wit and Humor of the Pennsylvania Germans*. Harrisburg, PA: The Author, 1946.

Ayre, Leslie. *The Wit of Music*. Boston, MA: Crescendo Publishing Company, 1969.

Banker, Stan. *Walk Cheerfully the Middleroad*. Richmond, IN: Friends United Press, 1994.

Barber, David W. *Bach, Beethoven, and the Boys*. Toronto, Canada: Sound and Vision, 1996.

Barber, David W. *When the Fat Lady Sings: Opera History as It Ought to be Taught*. Toronto, Canada: Sound and Vision, 1990.

Barnstone, Willis, translator. *Greek Lyric Poetry*. New York: Schocken Books, 1967.

Beach, Scott. *Musicdotes*. Berkeley, CA: Ten Speed Press, 1977.

Beecham, Thomas. A *Mingled Chime*. New York: Da Capo Press, 1976.

Benchley, Nathaniel. *Robert Benchley*. New York: McGraw-Hill Book Company, Inc., 1955.

Bernard, Catherine. *Sojourner Truth: Abolitionist and Women's Rights Activist*. Berkeley Heights, NJ: Enslow Publications, Inc., 2001.

Bing, Sir Rudolf. *5000 Nights at the Opera*. Garden City, NY: Doubleday and Company, Inc., 1972.

Blum, David. *Quintet: Five Journeys Toward Musical Fulfillment*. Ithaca, NY, and London: Cornell University Press, 1999.

Boxer, Tim. *The Jewish Celebrity Hall of Fame*. New York: Shapolsky Publishers, 1987.

Bracken, Peg. *But I Wouldn't Have Missed It for the World!* New York: Harcourt Brace Jovanovich, Inc., 1973.

Bracken, Peg. *The I Hate to Housekeep Book*. New York: Harcourt, Brace and World, Inc., 1962.

Brady, Logan Munger. *Amusing Anecdotes: Humorous Stories With a Moral*. Ann Arbor, MI: Ann Arbor Book Company, 1993.

Brandreth, Gyles. *Great Theatrical Disasters*. New York: St. Martin's Press, 1982.

Briggs, Joe Bob. *Profoundly Disturbing: Shocking Movies That Changed History!* New York: Universe Books, 2003.

Brown, Michèle and Ann O'Connor. *Hammer and Tongues: A Dictionary of Women's Wit and Humour*. London: J.M. Dent and Sons, Ltd., 1986.

Bryan III, J. *Merry Gentlemen (and One Lady)*. New York: Atheneum, 1985.

Brunsting, Bernard R. *Laugh!!! Your Health May Depend on It*. Columbus, GA: Quill Publications, 1995.

Burke, John. *Rogue's Progress: The Fabulous Adventures of Wilson Mizner*. New York: G.P. Putnam's Sons, 1975.

Cantor, Eddie, and David Freedman. *Ziegfeld: The Great Glorifier*. New York: Alfred H. King, Inc., 1934.

Charles, Helen White, collector and editor. *Quaker Chuckles and Other True Stories About Friends*. Oxford, OH: H.W. Charles, 1961.

Cleary, Thomas, translator. *Zen Antics: A Hundred Stories of Enlightenment*. Boston, MA: Shambhala Publications, Inc., 1993.

Clercq, Tanaquil Le. *The Ballet Cook Book*. New York: Stein and Day, Publishers, 1966.

Clower, Jerry. *Let the Hammer Down!* With Gerry Wood. Waco, TX: Word Books, Publisher, 1979.

Clower, Jerry. *Stories from Home*. Jackson, MS: University Press of Mississippi, 1992.

Cowan, Lore and Maurice. *The Wit of the Jews*. Nashville, TN: Aurora Publishers, Limited, 1970.

Crampton, Nancy, photographer. *Writers*. New York: The Quantuck Lane Press, 2005.

Deffaw, Chip. *Jazz Veterans: A Portrait Gallery*. Photographs by Nancy Miller Elliott and John & Andreas Johnsen. Fort Bragg, CA: Cypress House Press, 1996.

Denver, Bob. *Gilligan, Maynard and Me*. New York: Carol Publishing Group, 1993.

Donaldson, William. *Great Disasters of the Stage*. London: Arrow Books, Limited, 1984.

Downing, Charles. *Tales of the Hodja*. New York: Henry Z. Walck, Inc., 1965.

Eichenbaum, Rose. *Masters of Movement: Portraits of America's Great Choreographers*. Washington DC: Smithsonian Books, 2004.

Erskine, Carl. *Carl Erskine's Tales from the Dodger Dugout*. Champaigne, IL: Sports Publishing Inc., 2000.

Ford, Corey. *The Time of Laughter*. Boston, MA: Little, Brown and Company, 1967.

Fountain, Richard, compiler. *The Wit of the Wig*. London: Leslie Frewin Publishers, Limited, 1968.

Franklin, Joe. *Up Late with Joe Franklin*. New York: Scribner, 1995.

Furst, Herbert. *The New Anecdotes of Painters and Paintings*. London: The Bodley Head, Ltd., 1926.

Garner, Joe. *Made You Laugh: the Funniest Moments in Radio, Television, Stand-up, and Movie Comedy*. Kansas City, MO: Andrews McMeel Publishing, 2004.

Garner, Joe. *Now Showing: Unforgettable Moments from the Movies*. Kansas City, MO: Andrews McMeel Publishing, 2003.

Gaster, Moses. *The Exempla of the Rabbis: Being a Collection of Exempla, Apologues and Tales Culled from Hebrew Manuscripts and Rare Hebrew Books*. New York: Ktav Publishing House, Inc., 1968.

Gielgud, John. *Distinguished Company*. London: Heinemann, 1972.

Gielgud, John. *Stage Directions*. New York: Random House, 1963.

Goldin, Barbara Diamond. *A Child's Book of the Midrash: 52 Jewish Stories from the Sages*. Northvale, NJ: Jason Aronson. Inc., 1990.

Gray, Hector. *An Actor Looks Back*. Hobart Tasmania: Cat and Fiddle Press, 1973.

Greenberg, Jan, and Sandra Jordan. *Andy Warhol: Prince of Pop*. New York: Delacorte Press, 2004.

Greenberg, Jan and Sandra Jordan. *The Painter's Eye: Learning to Look at Contemporary American Art*. New York: Delacorte Press, 1991.

Greenberg, Steve, and Dale Ratermann. *I Remember Woody: Recollections of the Man They Called Coach Hayes*. Indianapolis, IN: Masters Press, 1997.

Greenfield, Lauren. *Girl Culture*. San Francisco, CA: Chronicle Books, 2002.

Grobel, Lawrence. *Above the Line: Conversations About the Movies*. N.p.: Da Capo Press, 2000.

Hall, Marilyn, and Rabbi Jerome Cutler. *The Celebrity Kosher Cookbook*. Los Angeles, CA: J.P. Tarcher, Inc., 1975.

Halliwell, Leslie. *The Filmgoer's Book of Quotes*. New Rochelle, NY: Arlington House Publishers, 1973.

Hecht, Ben. *Charlie: The Improbable Life and Times of Charles MacArthur*. New York: Harper & Brothers, Publishers, 1957.

Henry, Lewis C. *Humorous Anecdotes About Famous People*. Garden City, NY: Halcyon House, 1948.

Himelstein, Shmuel. *A Touch of Wisdom, A Touch of Wit*. Brooklyn, NY: Mesorah Publications, Limited, 1991.

Himelstein, Shmuel. *Words of Wisdom, Words of Wit*. Brooklyn, NY: Mesorah Publications, Ltd., 1993.

Holloway, Stanley. *Wiv a Little Bit O' Luck*. As told to Dick Richards. New York: Stein and Day, Publishers, 1967.

Hope, Bob. With Bob Thomas. *The Road to Hollywood: My Forty-Year Love Affair With the Movies*. Garden City, NY: Doubleday & Company, Inc., 1977.

Irving, Gordon, compiler. *The Wit of the Scots*. London: Leslie Frewin Publishers, Inc., 1969.

Javna, John. *The Best of TV Sitcoms*. New York: Harmony Books, 1988.

Johnson, Russell, and Steve Cox. *Here on Gilligan's Isle*. New York: HarperCollins Publishers, Inc., 1993.

Josephson, Judith Pinkerton. *Mother Jones: Fierce Fighter for Workers' Rights*. Minneapolis, MN: Lerner Publications Company, 1997.

Juno, Andrea. *Angry Women in Rock: Volume One*. New York: Juno Books, 1996.

Kanner, Bernice. *The 100 Best TV Commercials ... and Why They Worked*. New York: Times Books, 1999.

Knotts, Don. *Barney Fife and Other Characters I Have Known*. With Robert Metz. New York: Berkley Boulevard Books, 1999.

Laskas, Jeanne Marie. *We Remember: Women Born at the Turn of the Century Tell the Stories of Their Lives*. Photographs by Lynn Johnson. New York: William Morrow and Company, 1999.

Leonard, Sheldon. *And the Show Goes On: Broadway and Hollywood Adventures*. New York: Limelight, 1994.

Linkletter, Art. *I Didn't Do It Alone: The Autobiography of Art Linkletter*. Ottawa, IL: Caroline House Publishers, Inc., 1980.

Linkletter, Art. *Women are My Favorite People*. Garden City, NY: Doubleday & Company, Inc., 1974.

Lufkin, Elise. *Found Dogs: Tales of Strays Who Landed on Their Feet*. Photographs by Diana Walker. Guilford, CT: The Lyons Press, 2005.

Macnee, Patrick. *The Avengers and Me.* With Dave Rogers. New York: TV Books, 1997.

Macnee, Patrick, and Marie Cameron. *Blind in One Ear: The Avenger Returns.* San Francisco, CA: Mercury House, Inc., 1989.

Marx, Arthur. *Not as a Crocodile.* New York: Harper & Brothers, Publishers, 1958.

Marx, Groucho. *Confessions of a Mangy Lover.* New York: Da Capo Press, 1997.

Marx, Maxine. *Growing Up with Chico.* New York: Limelight Editions, 1986.

Maser, Frederick E., and Robert Drew Simpson. *If Saddlebags Could Talk: Methodist Stories and Anecdotes.* Franklin, TN: Providence House Publishers, 1998.

Maverick, Jr., Maury. *Texas Iconoclast.* Edited by Allan O. Kownslar. Fort Worth, TX: Texas Christian University Press, 1997.

McCann, Sean, compiler. *The Wit of the Irish.* Nashville, TN: Aurora Publishers, Ltd., 1970.

McPhaul, John J. *Deadlines and Moneyshines: The Fabled World of Chicago Journalism.* Englewood Cliffs, NJ: Prentice-Hall, Inc. 1962.

McPhee, Nancy. *The Second Book of Insults.* Toronto, Canada: Van Nostrand Reinhold, Ltd., 1981.

Mendelsohn, S. Felix. *Let Laughter Ring.* Philadelphia: The Jewish Publication Society of America, 1941.

Metil, Luana, and Jace Townsend. *The Story of Karate: From Buddhism to Bruce Lee.* Minneapolis, MN: Lerner Publications Company, 1995.

Miller, Brandon Marie. *Buffalo Gals: Women of the Old West.* Minneapolis, MN: Lerner Publications Company, 1995.

Miller, Brandon Marie. *Just What the Doctor Ordered: The History of American Medicine.* Minneapolis, MN: Lerner Publications Company, 1997.

Mingo, Jack. *The Juicy Parts.* New York: The Berkley Publishing Group, 1996.

Molen, Sam. *Take 2 and Hit to Right.* Philadelphia, PA: Dorrance and Company, 1959.

Morley, Robert. *Around the World in Eighty-One Years.* London: Hodder & Stoughton, 1990.

Morley, Robert. *Robert Morley's Book of Bricks.* New York: G.P. Putnam's Sons, 1979.

Mott, Robert L. *Radio Live! Television Live!: Those Golden Days When Horses Were Coconuts.* Jefferson, NC: McFarland & Company, Inc., Publishers, 2000.

Nachman, Gerald. *Seriously Funny: The Rebel Comedians of the 1950s and 1960s.* New York: Pantheon Books, 2003.

Pearson, Hesketh. *Lives of the Wits.* New York: Harper & Row, Publishers, 1962.

Primack, Ben, adapter and editor. *The Ben Hecht Show: Impolitic Observations from the Freest Thinker of 1950s Television*. Jefferson, NC: McFarland & Company, Inc., Publishers, 1993.

Rayment, Tabitha. *99 Classroom Calamities ... And How to Avoid Them*. London: Continuum International Publishing Group, 2006.

Raphael, Amy. *Grrrls: Viva Rock Divas*. New York: St. Martin's Griffin, 1996.

Reynolds, Moira Davison. *Women Champions of Human Rights*. Jefferson, NC: McFarland and Company, Inc., 1991.

Richards, Dick, compiler. *The Wit of Noël Coward*. London: Leslie Frewin, 1968.

Richards, Dick, compiler. *The Wit of Peter Ustinov*. London: Leslie Frewin Publishers, Limited, 1969.

Rodriguez-Hunter, Suzanne. *Found Meals of the Lost Generation*. Boston, MA: Faber and Faber, 1994.

Rogers, Dave. *The Avengers*. London: Independent Television Books, Ltd., 1983.

Rogers, Stephen D., editor. *My First Year in the Classroom: 50 Stories That Celebrate the Good, the Bad, and the Unforgettable Moments*. Avon, MA: Adams Media, 2009.

Rosen, Michael J., editor. *Dog People: Writers and Artists on Canine Companionship*. New York: Artisan, 1995.

Rosten, Leo. *People I Have Loved, Known or Admired*. New York: McGraw-Hill Book Company, 1970.

Royce, Brenda Scott. *Hogan's Heroes*. Jefferson, NC: McFarland & Company, Inc., Publishers, 1993.

Rutkowska, Wanda. *Famous People in Anecdotes*. Warszawa: Wydawnictwa Szkolne i Pedagogiczne, 1977.

Shah, Idries. *The Exploits of the Incomparable Mulla Nasrudin*. New York: E.P. Dutton and Co., 1966.

Singer, Marilyn. *Cats to the Rescue*. New York: Henry Holt and Company, 2006.

Sommers, Michael A. *Richard Peck*. New York: The Rosen Publishing Group, 2004.

Spring, Albert. *M.E. Kerr*. New York: The Rosen Publishing Group, 2006.

Tanner, Stephen. *Opera Antics and Anecdotes*. Toronto, Canada: Sound and Vision, 1999.

Taylor, Glenhall. *Before Television: The Radio Years*. New York: A.S. Barnes and Company, 1979.

True, Cynthia. *American Scream: The Bill Hicks Story*. New York: HarperEntertainment, 2002.

Tsai, Chih-Chung (editor and illustrator) and Kok Kok Kiang (translator). *The Book of Zen*. Singapore: Asiapac, 1990.

Twerski, M.D., Rabbi Abraham J. *Do Unto Others: How Good Deeds Can Change Your Life*. Kansas City, MO: Andrews McMeel Publishing, 1997.

Van Dyke, Dick. *Those Funny Kids!* Garden City, NY: Doubleday and Company, Inc., 1975.

Voskressenski, Alexei D., compiler and editor. *Cranks, Knaves, and Jokers of the Celestial*. Translated from the Chinese by Alexei Voskressenski and Vladimir Larin. Commack, NY: Nova Science Publishers, Inc., 1997.

Wagner, Alan. *Prima Donnas and Other Wild Beasts*. Larchmont, NY: Argonaut Books, 1961.

Warren, Roz, editor. *Dyke Strippers: Lesbian Cartoonists A to Z*. Pittsburgh, PA: Cleis Press, Inc., 1995.

Waters, John. *Shock Value*. New York: Dell Publishing Company, Inc., 1981.

Wilde, Larry. *The Great Comedians*. Secaucus, NJ: The Citadel Press, 1968.

Appendix B: About the Author

It was a dark and stormy night. Suddenly a cry rang out, and on a hot summer night in 1954, Josephine, wife of Carl Bruce, gave birth to a boy — me. Unfortunately, this young married couple allowed Reuben Saturday, Josephine's brother, to name their first-born. Reuben, aka "The Joker," decided that Bruce was a nice name, so he decided to name me Bruce Bruce. I have gone by my middle name — David — ever since.

Being named Bruce David Bruce hasn't been all bad. Bank tellers remember me very quickly, so I don't often have to show an ID. It can be fun in charades, also. When I was a counselor as a teenager at Camp Echoing Hills in Warsaw, Ohio, a fellow counselor gave the signs for "sounds like" and "two words," then she pointed to a bruise on her leg twice. Bruise Bruise? Oh yeah, Bruce Bruce is the answer!

Uncle Reuben, by the way, gave me a haircut when I was in kindergarten. He cut my hair short and shaved a small bald spot on the back of my head. My mother wouldn't let me go to school until the bald spot grew out again.

Of all my brothers and sisters (six in all), I am the only transplant to Athens, Ohio. I was born in Newark, Ohio, and have lived all around Southeastern Ohio. However, I moved to Athens to go to Ohio University and have never left.

At Ohio U, I never could make up my mind whether to major in English or Philosophy, so I got a bachelor's degree with a double major in both areas, then I added a master's degree in English and a master's degree in Philosophy. Yes, I have my MAMA degree,

Currently, and for a long time to come (I eat fruits and veggies), I am spending my retirement writing books such as *Nadia Comaneci: Perfect 10*, *The Funniest People in Dance*, *Homer's* Iliad: *A Retelling in Prose*, and *William Shakespeare's* Othello: *A Retelling in Prose.*

If all goes well, I will publish one or two books a year for the rest of my life. (On the other hand, a good way to make God laugh is to tell Her your plans.)

By the way, my sister Brenda Kennedy writes romances such as *A New Beginning* and *Shattered Dreams.*

Appendix C: Some Books by David Bruce

Anecdote Collections

250 Anecdotes About Opera
250 Anecdotes About Religion
250 Anecdotes About Religion: Volume 2
250 Music Anecdotes
Be a Work of Art: 250 Anecdotes and Stories
Boredom is Anti-Life: 250 Anecdotes and Stories
The Coolest People in Art: 250 Anecdotes
The Coolest People in the Arts: 250 Anecdotes
The Coolest People in Books: 250 Anecdotes
The Coolest People in Comedy: 250 Anecdotes
Create, Then Take a Break: 250 Anecdotes
Don't Fear the Reaper: 250 Anecdotes
The Funniest People in Art: 250 Anecdotes
The Funniest People in Books: 250 Anecdotes
The Funniest People in Books, Volume 2: 250 Anecdotes
The Funniest People in Books, Volume 3: 250 Anecdotes
The Funniest People in Comedy: 250 Anecdotes
The Funniest People in Dance: 250 Anecdotes
The Funniest People in Families: 250 Anecdotes
The Funniest People in Families, Volume 2: 250 Anecdotes
The Funniest People in Families, Volume 3: 250 Anecdotes
The Funniest People in Families, Volume 4: 250 Anecdotes
The Funniest People in Families, Volume 5: 250 Anecdotes
The Funniest People in Families, Volume 6: 250 Anecdotes
The Funniest People in Movies: 250 Anecdotes
The Funniest People in Music: 250 Anecdotes
The Funniest People in Music, Volume 2: 250 Anecdotes
The Funniest People in Music, Volume 3: 250 Anecdotes
The Funniest People in Neighborhoods: 250 Anecdotes
The Funniest People in Relationships: 250 Anecdotes
The Funniest People in Sports: 250 Anecdotes
The Funniest People in Sports, Volume 2: 250 Anecdotes
The Funniest People in Television and Radio: 250 Anecdotes

The Funniest People in Theater: 250 Anecdotes
The Funniest People Who Live Life: 250 Anecdotes
The Funniest People Who Live Life, Volume 2: 250 Anecdotes
The Kindest People Who Do Good Deeds, Volume 1: 250 Anecdotes
The Kindest People Who Do Good Deeds, Volume 2: 250 Anecdotes
Maximum Cool: 250 Anecdotes
The Most Interesting People in Movies: 250 Anecdotes
The Most Interesting People in Politics and History: 250 Anecdotes
The Most Interesting People in Politics and History, Volume 2: 250 Anecdotes
The Most Interesting People in Politics and History, Volume 3: 250 Anecdotes
The Most Interesting People in Religion: 250 Anecdotes
The Most Interesting People in Sports: 250 Anecdotes
The Most Interesting People Who Live Life: 250 Anecdotes
The Most Interesting People Who Live Life, Volume 2: 250 Anecdotes
Reality is Fabulous: 250 Anecdotes and Stories
Resist Psychic Death: 250 Anecdotes

[1]Source: Judith Pinkerton Josephson, *Mother Jones: Fierce Fighter for Workers' Rights*, pp. 101-102.

[2]Source: Maury Maverick, Jr., *Texas Iconoclast*, p. 64.

[3]Source: Leslie Halliwell, *The Filmgoer's Book of Quotes*, pp. 3, 4, and 111.

[4]Source: Michèle Brown and Ann O'Connor, *Hammer and Tongues*, p. 154.

[5]Source: Gyles Brandreth, *Great Theatrical Disasters*, p. 105.

[6]Source: Patrick Macnee, *The Avengers and Me*, pp. 62-63.

[7] Source: John Gielgud, *Distinguished Company*, p. 17.

[8] Source: John Gielgud, *Stage Directions*, p. 51.

[9]Source: Joe Bob Briggs, *Profoundly Disturbing: Shocking Movies That Changed History!*, p. 208.

[10] Source: Joe Garner, *Made You Laugh*, pp. 49-50.

[11]Source: Bob Hope, *The Road to Hollywood*, p. 35.

[12]Source: Bernice Kanner, *The 100 Best TV Commercials*, pp. 157-158.

[13]Source: Glenhall Taylor, *Before Television*, pp. 20-21.

[14]Source: Patrick Macnee and Marie Cameron, *Blind in One Ear*, pp. 256-257.

[15] Source: Andrea Juno, *Angry Women in Rock: Volume One*, pp. 201-202.

[16]Source: Lore and Maurice Cowan, *The Wit of the Jews*, p. 15.

[17]Source: John Burke, *Rogue's Progress: The Fabulous Adventures of Wilson Mizner*, pp. 101-102.

[18]Source: David W. Barber, *When the Fat Lady Sings*, p. 33.

[19]Source: Stanley Holloway, *Wiv a Little Bit O' Luck*, p. 43.

[20] Source: Willis Barnstone, translator, *Greek Lyric Poetry*, p. 44.

[21]Source: Gordon Irving, compiler, *The Wit of the Scots*, pp. 96-97.

[22]Source: Sean McCann, compiler, *The Wit of the Irish*, p. 33.

[23]Source: Richard Fountain, compiler, *The Wit of the Wig*, p. 25.

[24] Source: Art Linkletter, *Women are My Favorite People*, p. 142.

[25] Source: Michael J. Rosen, editor, *Dog People: Writers and Artists on Canine Companionship*, p. 110.

[26]Source: Ben Primack, adapter and editor, *The Ben Hecht Show*, pp. 215-216.

[27]Source: Dick Richards, compiler, *The Wit of Peter Ustinov*, p. 110.

[28]Source: Jan Greenberg and Sandra Jordan, *Andy Warhol: Prince of Pop*, pp. 78-79.

[29]Source: Jack Mingo, *The Juicy Parts*, p. 80.

[30] Source: Carl Erskine, *Carl Erskine's Tales from the Dodger Dugout*, pp. 73-74.

[31] Source: Sam Molen, *Take 2 and Hit to Right*, pp. 12-13.

[32]Source: Dick Van Dyke, *Those Funny Kids!*, pp. 32, 34.

[33]Source: Jan Greenberg and Sandra Jordan, *The Painter's Eye*, p. 25.

[34] Source: Tanaquil Le Clercq, *The Ballet Cook Book*, p. 347

[35]Source: Thomas Cleary, translator, *Zen Antics*, p. 18.

[36] Source: Emine Saner, "Why I still get incredibly excited about Christmas." *The Guardian*. 9 December 2009 <http://www.guardian.co.uk/theguardian/2009/dec/09/christmas>.

[37] Source: Joe Franklin, *Up Late with Joe Franklin*, pp. 225-226.

[38] Source: Roger Ebert, "Siskel & Ebert & the Jugular." Blogs.suntimes.com. 19 November 2008 <http://blogs.suntimes.com/ebert/2008/11/siskel_ebert_the_jugular.html#more>.

[39]Source: Thomas Cleary, translator, *Zen Antics*, pp. 4-5.

[40] Source: John Gielgud, *Distinguished Company*, pp. 69-70.

[41]Source: Ben Hecht, *Charlie: The Improbable Life and Times of Charles MacArthur*, p. 140.

[42]Source: Leo Rosten, *People I Have Loved, Known or Admired*, p. 235.

[43]Source: Jeanne Marie Laskas, *We Remember*, p. 103.

[44]Source: Robert Morley, *Robert Morley's Book of Bricks*, p. 61.

[45]Source: Sheldon Leonard, *And the Show Goes On*, pp. 96-98.

[46] Source: Joe Franklin, *Up Late with Joe Franklin*, pp. 185-186.

[47]Source: Gerald Nachman, *Seriously Funny*, p. 382.

[48]Source: Tim Boxer, *The Jewish Celebrity Hall of Fame*, p. 85.

[49]Source: Robert L. Mott, *Radio Live! Television Live!*, p. 167.

[50]Source: Bob Hope, *The Road to Hollywood*, pp. 16-17.

[51]Source: Art Linkletter, *I Didn't Do It Alone*, p. 173.

[52]Source: Shmuel Himelstein, *Words of Wisdom, Words of Wit*, p. 262.

[53]Source: John Waters, *Shock Value*, pp. 67, 152.

[54] Source: John Burke, *Rogue's Progress: The Fabulous Adventures of Wilson Mizner*, p. 260.

[55] Source: Thomas Beecham, *A Mingled Chime*, pp. 136-137.

[56] Source: Sir Rudolf Bing, *5000 Nights at the Opera*, p. 14.

[57] Source: Roz Warren, editor, *Dyke Strippers: Lesbian Cartoonists A to Z*, p. 21.

[58] Source: Jan Greenberg and Sandra Jordan, *Andy Warhol: Prince of Pop*, pp. 11, 96, 118.

[59] Source: David W. Barber, *Bach, Beethoven, and the Boys*, pp. 81-82.

[60] Source: Sheldon Leonard, *And the Show Goes On*, pp. 20-21.

[61] Source: Hector Gray, *An Actor Looks Back*, p. 24.

[62] Source: Nancy McPhee, *The Second Book of Insults*, p. 125.

[63] Source: Shams al-Din Ahmad Aflaki, *Legends of the Sufis*, p. 83.

[64] Source: Jerry Clower, *Let the Hammer Down!*, p. 63.

[65] Source: Tabitha Rayment, *99 Classroom Calamities ... And How to Avoid Them*, pp. 8-9, 44, 62.

[66] Source: Stephen D. Rogers, editor, *My First Year in the Classroom: 50 Stories That Celebrate the Good, the Bad, and the Unforgettable Moments*, pp. 125-126.

[67] Source: Bob Denver, *Gilligan, Maynard and Me*, p. 67.

[68] Source: Merrill Ashley, *Dancing for Balanchine*, pp. 32, 34.

[69] Source: Albert Spring, *M.E. Kerr*, p. 19.

[70] Source: Jan Greenberg and Sandra Jordan, *The Painter's Eye*, p. 66.

[71] Source: Dick Van Dyke, *Those Funny Kids!*, pp. 63-64.

[72] Source: "20 Questions: Steve Wynn." March 2008 <http://www.popmatters.com/pm/features/article/55816/steve-wynn/>.

[73] Source: David Blum, *Quintet: Five Journeys Toward Musical Fulfillment*, p. 96.

[74] Source: Shams al-Din Ahmad Aflaki, *Legends of the Sufis*, p. 55.

[75] Source: Russell Johnson and Steve Cox, *Here on Gilligan's Isle*, p. 176.

[76] Source: Tim Boxer, *The Jewish Celebrity Hall of Fame*, p. 228.

[77] Source: Larry Wilde, *The Great Comedians*, p. 27.

[78] Source: Herbert Furst, *The New Anecdotes of Painters and Paintings*, p. 58.

[79] Source: Luana Metil and Jace Townsend, *The Story of Karate: From Buddhism to Bruce Lee*, pp. 65, 95-96.

[80] Source: Sam Molen, *Take 2 and Hit to Right*, pp. 16-17.

[81] Source: Steve Greenberg and Dale Ratermann, *I Remember Woody: Recollections of the Man They Called Coach Hayes*, p. 200.

[82] Source: Bernice Kanner, *The 100 Best TV Commercials*, p. 159.

[83] Source: Hesketh Pearson, *Lives of the Wits*, p. 179.

[84] Source: John Javna, *The Best of TV Sitcoms*, p. 126.

[85] Source: Albert Spring, *M.E. Kerr*, p. 11

[86] Source: Karen Adir, *The Great Clowns of American Television*, p. 120.

[87] Source: Tanaquil Le Clercq, *The Ballet Cook Book*, p. 410.

[88] Source: Sean McCann, compiler, *The Wit of the Irish*, p. 66.

[89] Source: Bill Adler, *Jewish Wit and Wisdom*, pp. 69-70.

[90] Source: Roz Warren, editor, *Dyke Strippers: Lesbian Cartoonists A to Z*, p. 38.

[91] Source: Cynthia True, *American Scream: The Bill Hicks Story*, pp. 154, 181.

[92] Source: Groucho Marx, *Confessions of a Mangy Lover*, pp. 131ff.

[93] Source: Maxine Marx, *Growing Up with Chico*, pp. 57-58.

[94] Source: Logan Munger Brady, *Amusing Anecdotes*, p. 186.

[95] Source: Richard Fountain, compiler, *The Wit of the Wig*, pp. 19-20.

[96] Source: J. Bryan III, *Merry Gentlemen (and One Lady)*, p. 83.

[97] Source: John Gielgud, *Distinguished Company*, p. 62.

[98] Source: "Why Ben & Jerry's Honored Marriage Equality." *The Advocate*. 2 September 2009 <http://www.advocate.com/Business/Why_Ben__amp;_Jerry__39;s_Honored_Marriage_Equality/>.

[99] Source: Marilyn Singer, *Cats to the Rescue*, pp. 69-70.

[100] Source: Elise Lufkin, *Found Dogs: Tales of Strays Who Landed on Their Feet*, pp. 58-59.

[101] Source: John J. McPhaul, *Deadlines and Moneyshines: The Fabled World of Chicago Journalism*, p. 289.

[102] Source: Hadley Freeman, "America is the true home of Halloween." *The Guardian*. 30 October 2009 <http://www.guardian.co.uk/lifeandstyle/2009/oct/30/america-halloween-trick-treat>.

[103] Source: Rabbi Abraham J. Twerski, M.D., *Do Unto Others: How Good Deeds Can Change Your Life*, pp. 93-94.

[104] Source: Frederick E. Maser and Robert Drew Simpson, *If Saddlebags Could Talk*, p. 33.

[105] Source: "20 Questions: Thomas Dolby." Popmatters.com. 9 June 2008 <http://www.popmatters.com/pm/features/article/59529/thomas-dolby/>.

[106] Source: Peg Bracken, *The I Hate to Housekeep Book*, p. 11.

[107] Source: Marilyn Singer, *Cats to the Rescue*, pp. 93-95.

[108] Source: Jeanne Marie Laskas, *We Remember*, p. 40.

[109] Source: Brandon Marie Miller, *Just What the Doctor Ordered: The History of American Medicine*, pp. 42, 44.

[110] Source: Stanley Holloway, *Wiv a Little Bit O' Luck*, p. 168.

[111] Source: Idries Shah, *The Exploits of the Incomparable Nasrudin*, p. 28.

[112] Source: Hesketh Pearson, *Lives of the Wits*, p. 99.

[113] Source: Stephen Tanner, *Opera Antics and Anecdotes*, p. 106.

[114] Source: Corey Ford, *The Time of Laughter*, p. 63.

[115] Source: Lewis C. Henry, *Humorous Anecdotes About Famous People*, p. 89.

[116] Source: Charles Downing, *Tales of the Hodja*, pp. 3, 82.

[117] Source: Frederick E. Maser and Robert Drew Simpson, *If Saddlebags Could Talk*, pp. 98-100.

[118] Source: Gordon Irving, compiler, *The Wit of the Scots*, p. 56.

[119] Source: Sir Rudolf Bing, *5000 Nights at the Opera*, pp. 41-42.

[120] Source: Arthur Marx, *Not as a Crocodile*, pp. 97-103.

[121] Source: Nancy Crampton, photographer, *Writers*, pp. 62-63.

[122] Source: Russell Johnson and Steve Cox, *Here on Gilligan's Isle*, p. 185.

[123] Source: Nancy McPhee, *The Second Book of Insults*, p. 46.

[124] Source: John J. McPhaul, *Deadlines and Moneyshines: The Fabled World of Chicago Journalism*, pp. 12-13.

[125] Source: John Waters, *Shock Value*, p. 46.

[126] Source: Brandon Marie Miller, *Just What the Doctor Ordered: The History of American Medicine*, p. 57.

[127] Source: Roger Ebert, "The good are always the merry." 31 May 2009 <http://blogs.suntimes.com/ebert/2009/05/ and_say_my_glory_was_i_had_suc.html>.

[128] Source: Robert Morley, *Robert Morley's Book of Bricks*, p. 90.

[129] Source: Stephen Tanner, *Opera Antics and Anecdotes*, pp. 22-23, 112.

[130] Source: Gyles Brandreth, *Great Theatrical Disasters*, p. 18.

[131] Source: Harold Atkins and Archie Newman, *Beecham Stories*, p. 29.

[132] Source: Nancy Crampton, photographer, *Writers*, pp. 60-61.

[133] Source: Don Knotts, *Barney Fife and Other Characters I Have Known*, pp. 216-217.

[134] Source: Art Linkletter, *Women are My Favorite People*, p. 126.

[135] Source: Stephen D. Rogers, editor, *My First Year in the Classroom: 50 Stories That Celebrate the Good, the Bad, and the Unforgettable Moments*, p. 151.

[136] Source: Robert Morley, *Around the World in Eighty-One Years*, p. 78.

[137] Source: Eve Arden, *Three Phases of Eve*, p. 22.

[138] Source: William Donaldson, *Great Disasters of the Stage*, p. 13.

[139] Source: Moses Gaster, *The Exempla of the Rabbis*, p. 138.

[140] Source: Alexei D. Voskressenski, compiler and editor, *Cranks, Knaves, and Jokers of the Celestial*, pp. 14-15.

[141] Source: Bill Adler, *Jewish Wit and Wisdom*, pp. 36-37.

[142] Source: Lauren Greenfield, *Girl Culture*, p. 42.

[143] Source: Carl Erskine, *Carl Erskine's Tales from the Dodger Dugout*, pp. 87-88.

[144] Source: Joe Garner, *Now Showing: Unforgettable Moments from the Movies*, p. 75.

[145] Source: Thomas Beecham, *A Mingled Chime*, pp. 316-317.

[146] Source: S. Felix Mendelsohn, *Let Laughter Ring*, p. 62. Also: Source: Hesketh Pearson, *Lives of the Wits*, p. 140.

[147] Source: Mark Shields, "What Joseph Heller Could Teach Wall Street." Creators Syndicate. 28 November 2009 <http://www.creators.com/liberal/mark-shields/what-joseph-heller-could-teach-wall-street.html>.

[148] Source: Jerry Clower, *Stories from Home*, p. 7.

[149] Source: Alan Wagner, *Prima Donnas and Other Wild Beasts*, pp. 12-13.

[150] Source: Eddie Cantor and David Freedman, *Ziegfeld: The Great Glorifier*, p. 24.

[151]Source: Chih-Chung Tsai (editor and illustrator) and Kok Kok Kiang (translator), *The Book of Zen*, p. 66.

[152]Source: Shmuel Himelstein, *A Touch of Wisdom, A Touch of Wit*, p. 203.

[153]Source: Wanda Rutkowska, *Famous People in Anecdotes*, p. 65.

[154]Source: Luana Metil and Jace Townsend, *The Story of Karate: From Buddhism to Bruce Lee*, pp. 82-83.

[155]Source: J. Bryan III, *Merry Gentlemen (and One Lady)*, p. 26.

[156]Source: Bernard R. Brunsting, *Laugh!!! Your Health May Depend on It*, p. 32.

[157]Source: Charles Downing, *Tales of the Hodja*, p. 3.

[158]Source: Leslie Ayre, *The Wit of Music*, p. 48.

[159]Source: Peg Bracken, *But I Wouldn't Have Missed It for the World!*, p. 152.

[160]Source: Moses Gaster, *The Exempla of the Rabbis*, p. 96.

[161]Source: Maury Maverick, Jr., *Texas Iconoclast*, p. 62.

[162]Source: Joe Bob Briggs, *Profoundly Disturbing: Shocking Movies That Changed History!*, p. 236.

[163] Source: Karen Adir, *The Great Clowns of American Television*, p. 149.

[164]Source: Leslie Halliwell, *The Filmgoer's Book of Quotes*, Foreword.

[165]Source: Joe Garner, *Now Showing: Unforgettable Moments from the Movies*, p. 72.

[166] Source: Amy Raphael, *Grrrls: Viva Rock Divas*, pp. 202, 205-206.

[167]Source: Frances Alda, *Men, Women, and Tenors*, pp. 186-188.

[168]Source: Corey Ford, *The Time of Laughter*, p. 16.

[169] Source: Andrea Juno, *Angry Women in Rock: Volume One*, p. 79.

[170]Source: Scott Beach, *Musicdotes*, p. 82.

[171] Source: Chip Deffaw, *Jazz Veterans: A Portrait Gallery*, p. 190.

[172]Source: David W. Barber, *When the Fat Lady Sings*, pp. 100-101.

[173]Source: Ken Alley, *Awkward Christian Soldiers*, p. 46.

[174] Source: Maxine Marx, *Growing Up with Chico*, p. 38.

[175]Source: Moira Davison Reynolds, *Women Champions of Human Rights*, p. 41.

[176]Source: Nathaniel Benchley, *Robert Benchley*, p. 28.

[177] Source: John Dickerson, "The Better To-Do List." *Slate*. 12 October 2009 <http://www.slate.com/id/2231911/>.

[178]Source: Marilyn Hall and Rabbi Jerome Cutler, *The Celebrity Kosher Cookbook*, p. 98.

[179]Source: Bernard R. Brunsting, *Laugh!!! Your Health May Depend on It*, p. 100.

[180]Source: Eve Arden, *Three Phases of Eve*, p. 51.

[181]Source: Judith Pinkerton Josephson, *Mother Jones: Fierce Fighter for Workers' Rights*, p. 115.

[182] Source: Lawrence Grobel, *Above the Line: Conversations About the Movies*, p. 354.

[183]Source: Brenda Scott Royce, *Hogan's Heroes*, pp. 30, 32.

[184]Source: Glenhall Taylor, *Before Television*, pp. 124, 126.

[185]Source: Scott Beach, *Musicdotes*, p. 53.

[186] Source: Connie Schultz, "Never Trust a Viral Prayer." Creators Syndicate. 23 September 2009 <http://www.creators.com/liberal/connie-schultz/never-trust-a-viral-prayer.html>.

[187]Source: Joey Adams, *The God Bit*, p. 31.

[188] Source: Amy Raphael, *Grrrls: Viva Rock Divas*, p. 90.

[189] Source: Chip Deffaw, *Jazz Veterans: A Portrait Gallery*, p. 41.

[190]Source: Barbara Diamond Goldin, *A Child's Book of the Midrash: 52 Jewish Stories from the Sages*, pp. 16-19.

[191]Source: Frances Alda, *Men, Women, and Tenors*, p. 152.

[192]Source: Catherine Bernard, *Sojourner Truth: Abolitionist and Women's Rights Activist*, pp. 87-88.

[193]Source: Brandon Marie Miller, *Buffalo Gals: Women of the Old West*, pp. 13-14, 19.

[194] Source: Michael J. Rosen, editor, *Dog People: Writers and Artists on Canine Companionship*, p. 134.

[195]Source: Moira Davison Reynolds, *Women Champions of Human Rights*, p. 63.

[196] Source: Steve Greenberg and Dale Ratermann, *I Remember Woody: Recollections of the Man They Called Coach Hayes*, pp. 129-130.

[197]Source: Wanda Rutkowska, *Famous People in Anecdotes*, p. 49.

[198]Source: Jack Mingo, *The Juicy Parts*, p. 158.

[199]Source: Alan Wagner, *Prima Donnas and Other Wild Beasts*, p. 226.

[200]Source: Peg Bracken, *The I Hate to Housekeep Book*, p. 59.

[201]Source: Brenda Scott Royce, *Hogan's Heroes*, p. 117.

[202]Source: Helen White Charles, collector and editor, *Quaker Chuckles*, pp. 28-29.

[203]Source: Joey Adams, *The God Bit*, p. 291.

[204]Source: Michèle Brown and Ann O'Connor, *Hammer and Tongues*, p. 110.

[205]Source: Leo Rosten, *People I Have Loved, Known or Admired*, p. 97.

[206] Source: Eddie Cantor and David Freedman, *Ziegfeld: The Great Glorifier*, pp. 36-39.

[207]Source: Art Linkletter, *I Didn't Do It Alone*, pp. 69-70.

[208]Source: Stan Banker, *Walk Cheerfully the Middleroad*, cover and p. 145.

[209]Source: Helen White Charles, collector and editor, *Quaker Chuckles*, p. 26.

[210]Source: Barbara Diamond Goldin, *A Child's Book of the Midrash: 52 Jewish Stories from the Sages*, pp. 47-50.

[211] Source: Rabbi Abraham J. Twerski, M.D., *Do Unto Others: How Good Deeds Can Change Your Life*, p. 136.

[212] Source: S. Felix Mendelsohn, *Let Laughter Ring*, p. 50.

[213]Source: Ben Primack, adapter and editor, *The Ben Hecht Show*, pp. 122-123.

[214]Source: Logan Munger Brady, *Amusing Anecdotes*, p. 34.

[215]Source: Leslie Ayre, *The Wit of Music*, p. 45.

[216]Source: Patrick Macnee and Marie Cameron, *Blind in One Ear*, p. 173.

[217]Source: Dave Rogers, *The Avengers*, p. 77.

[218]Source: Bob Denver, *Gilligan, Maynard and Me*, p. 112.

[219]Source: Patrick Macnee, *The Avengers and Me*, pp. 75, 78.

[220]Source: John Javna, *The Best of TV Sitcoms*, p. 48.

[221] Source: Elise Lufkin, *Found Dogs: Tales of Strays Who Landed on Their Feet*, pp. 72-73.

[222]Source: Dick Richards, compiler, *The Wit of Peter Ustinov*, p. 18.

[223]Source: Dick Richards, compiler, *The Wit of Noël Coward*, p. 39.

[224] Source: Michael A. Sommers, *Richard Peck*, pp. 17, 20.

[225] Source: David Blum, *Quintet: Five Journeys Toward Musical Fulfillment*, p. 35.

[226] Source: Rose Eichenbaum, *Masters of Movement: Portraits of America's Great Choreographers*, p. 179.

[227] Source: Lewis C. Henry, *Humorous Anecdotes About Famous People*, p. 108.

[228] Source: Brandon Marie Miller, *Buffalo Gals: Women of the Old West*, p. 27.

[229] Source: Peg Bracken, *But I Wouldn't Have Missed It for the World!*, p. 42.

[230] Source: Shmuel Himelstein, *A Touch of Wisdom, A Touch of Wit*, p. 221.

[231] Source: Alexei D. Voskressenski, compiler and editor, *Cranks, Knaves, and Jokers of the Celestial*, p. 11.

[232] Source: Shmuel Himelstein, *Words of Wisdom, Words of Wit*, p. 53.

[233] Source: Harold Atkins and Archie Newman, *Beecham Stories*, pp. 30, 65, 67-68.

[234] Source: Ben Hecht, *Charlie: The Improbable Life and Times of Charles MacArthur*, pp. 18-19.

[235] Source: Lauren Greenfield, *Girl Culture*, p. 32.

[236] Source: Michael A. Sommers, *Richard Peck*, pp. 25-26.

[237] Source: Merrill Ashley, *Dancing for Balanchine*, p. 100.

[238] Source: Nathaniel Benchley, *Robert Benchley*, p. 8.

[239] Source: Rose Eichenbaum, *Masters of Movement: Portraits of America's Great Choreographers*, p. 134.

[240] Source: Herbert Furst, *The New Anecdotes of Painters and Paintings*, pp. 20-21.

[241] Source: Gerald Nachman, *Seriously Funny*, p. 28.

[242] Source: Lawrence Grobel, *Above the Line: Conversations About the Movies*, pp. 221-222.

[243] Source: David W. Barber, *Bach, Beethoven, and the Boys*, p. 50.

[244] Source: Robert Morley, *Around the World in Eighty-One Years*, p. 48.

[245] Source: William Donaldson, *Great Disasters of the Stage*, pp. 88-89.

[246] Source: Robert L. Mott, *Radio Live! Television Live!*, p. 162.

[247] Source: Ken Alley, *Awkward Christian Soldiers*, p. 90.

[248] Source: Joe Garner, *Made You Laugh*, p. 10.

[249] Source: Dick Richards, compiler, *The Wit of Noël Coward*, p. 60.

[250] Source: Lore and Maurice Cowan, *The Wit of the Jews*, p. 84.

9 798215 871140